PICKLEBALL LEADERSHIP

LESSONS FROM THE COURT TO THE BOARDROOM

KALIYM A. ISLAM, PH.D.

TRAININGPRO ACADEMY PRESS

DEDICATION

This book is dedicated to my tribe, my peeps, my crew;
the group of strangers who became family; the FishhawkPickle-
ball Club, Lithia Florida.

CONTENTS

PREFACE

I remember the first time I heard the word "pickleball." I was in a cigar lounge, sitting at a table with a client, when I overheard two gentlemen (at a table next to us) having an enthusiastic conversation about "banging," "poaching," and "pickling." I apologized for ease-dropping on their discussion and inquired about the sport they were talking about. Their eyes opened wide with excitement as they raved about pickleball and tried to explain its complicated rules.

The cigar aficionados couldn't hide their enthusiasm for the game as they took turns attempting to describe the nuances of pickleball, and how it was a cross between tennis, ping-pong, and chess. When the conversation ended I couldn't help but think "those guys sound like their part of a cult." But... something about the discussion intrigued me.

I went home that evening, googled pickleball, and started watching some instructional videos. The game seemed like fun. And, after three back surgeries, due of the wear and tear on my body from CrossFit and golf, I was looking for a new athletic challenge to keep me busy. The next day I went to Walmart and purchased a "starter" pickleball set for $19.99.

I also searched the internet to find pickleball courts in my area and located a park on Nature's Way in Valrico Florida. I showed up wearing Khakis, a Polo shirt, and cross trainers. Looking back, I must have been a sight to see for these "seasoned" pickleball players. The park had two sets of courts. Two were dedicated for pickleball and were enclosed by a fence. There were also and two tennis courts that had pickleball lines painted on them. I would later learn that the dedicated pickleball courts were referred to as "the cage."

I didn't know a lot about the sport at the time, but I could tell that the athletes who played in the "cage" we're at a different level than those who played on the tennis courts. So...I decided I should probably start on the tennis courts. As soon as I stepped onto the tennis court one of the players, who were waiting to play in the cage, a chiropractor named Michelle, came over and introduced herself. She asked what I knew about the game and how long I'd been playing. My answers were "not a lot" and "this is my first time."

Although I never played before I was an athlete who could get to most shots and return the ball to the other side of the net...although not with a lot of accuracy. After beating a few of my fellow "tennis court" pickleball players my confidence was up and I decided to take a chance and play in the "cage." I put my paddle in the paddle holder and waited my turn. After a few minutes I heard "next four up." I looked to see where the announcement was coming from and saw a athletic looking man holding up four paddles, including my own, while looking to see who would come forward to play.

The gentleman holding the paddles was a tall, friendly, distinguished looking athlete named Brian Grant. I would later learn that Brian was a pickleball coach and arguably one of the best players in a hundred mile radius. As he handed each of the "next four" their paddles, Brian looked at me and said "You probably don't want to play with that paddle. I've got one that's better." He reached into his bag and handed me a black paddle with the word "Engage" written on it.

Well...the updated paddle didn't help my game much. My opponents moved me back and forth, left and right, and deposited many of my feeble shot attempts back into my chest, legs, and feet. Exhausted, but determined to get better, I left the court vowing to myself that I'd get better. As I handed Brian back his paddle, I overheard another pickleballplayer, a woman who everyone called "Sassy," mention that there were pickleball courts in the neighborhood where I lived; Fishhawk.

My plan was set. I would go to the pickleball courts in Fishhawk which according to Sassy weren't as crowded, practice my game, get better, and then come back to dominate the "Nature's Way Crew".

My First Pickleball Leadership Lesson

After playing pickleball (at the Fishhawk courts) for about two months, my khakis and polo shirt were replaced by dry fit shorts and tee's along with KSwiss pickleball sneakers. I was officially part of the cult. During that eight week period I also made the mandatory pilgrimage to the "Engage" Pickleball Factory, where I purchased a refurbished Pursuit Pro MX and donated my starter kit paddles to one of the new players who showed up at the court without equipment. And, my game had improved. My serve was decent and I was missing fewer "easy" shots. That's when I got my first lesson on the relationship between pickleball and leadership.

I was playing a game of mixed doubles when one of my opponents, a tall, athletic, distinguished looking woman named Amber deposited one of my ill advised pop up shots directly into my chest. Amber smiled and said "sorry, but not sorry." The scenario happened two or three more times during the game. After, I joked with Amber by saying "I thought we were friends." Amber flashed her infectious smile again and said "well Kaliym, if you don't want the ball hit at you like that, don't put the ball where you put it."

For some reason, that statement hit me like a ton of bricks. Instead of thinking about Amber's response in pickleballterms, I kept thinking about the times (during my leadership career) where bad things happened not so much as a result of what someone else did, but because I didn't position myself correctly or made decisions (akin to hitting a pop up shot) that allowed bad things to happen.

The more I pondered the nuances of pickleball including the shot selections, the communication and the positioning, the more I saw the parallels between how great pickleball players play and how great leaders lead. This personal awakening was the catalyst for this book.

Reading "Pickleball Leadership: Lessons From The Court to The Boardroom" is not just about acquiring knowledge; it's about embarking on a transformative journey that can have a profound impact on your personal and professional life. So, get ready to embark on a journey that merges the principles of sportsmanship, strategy, and leadership that provides you with the tools and inspiration needed to become a more effective and impactful leader. As you apply these lessons from the court to the boardroom, you'll not only elevate your leadership skills but also enhance your overall quality of life. Get ready to step onto the court of leadership excellence and emerge as a visionary leader in your field.

CHAPTER ONE

INTRODUCTION

W elcome to the exciting world of Pickleball Leadership! Join us as we embark on a journey that blends sportsmanship and leadership. Pickleball, a paddle sport that combines elements of tennis, badminton, and ping pong, has surged in popularity over the years. Its fast-paced nature demands quick thinking, strategic planning, and precise execution. As players engage in dynamic court battles, they also embody qualities crucial to leadership: communication, collaboration, decision-making under pressure, and the ability to learn and evolve. Just as a successful pickleball player must anticipate their opponent's moves and adjust their strategy on the fly, effective leaders must navigate challenges with agility and foresight, constantly refining their approach to achieve their goals.

Pickleball's fast-paced fun and dynamic strategies mirror the everyday challenges leaders encounter. The court becomes a metaphorical testing ground, teaching important qualities like precision, adaptability, teamwork, and unwavering determination. These traits are just as essential for success in the business world and beyond.

Through the engaging stories of leaders, we'll uncover the connections between their pickleball experiences and their leadership successes. Each chapter will showcase a leader's journey, revealing how they navigated their careers' twists and turns, much like they maneuver on the pickleball court.

Get ready to be inspired as we explore the valuable lessons from pickleball that they've seamlessly applied to real-life leadership situations. Whether you're an experienced leader seeking fresh perspectives or an aspiring leader looking to develop skills, this book offers transformative insights.

So, let's dive into the lives of these outstanding leaders and see how they've used the pickleball spirit to achieve triumphs in their leadership roles!

CHAPTER TWO

THE SERVE OF INFLUENCE

INSPIRING TEAMS TO GREATNESS

This chapter goes into the heart of leadership, which is all about serving and influencing others. This is where we dive into how being a leader is like serving in pickleball—it's a big deal that affects everything that comes after.

The serve in pickleball can totally control a rally, and leaders' first moves can heavily impact their team's morale, dynamic, and overall path. Leaders who are present, set a positive tone, and inspire their team can drive them to achieve greatness.

As we explore the parallels between the serve's ripple effect in pickleball and leadership's influence, prepare to examine the nuances of presence, communication, and motivational prowess. Join us in deciphering how the serve of influence, much like the serve in pickleball, not only starts the game but lays the groundwork for an exceptional journey of collaboration, growth, and remarkable achievements.

What is The Pickleball Serve?

The serve starts every pickleball game and begins every pickleball rally. It plays a crucial role in determining the strategy of the game, and influences not only the momentum, but also the dynamics of the competition. A well-executed service can set the mood, create strategic positioning opportunities and force your opponent(s) to react according to its speed, trajectory, and spin.

Players often use the serve to leverage their own strengths and exploit the weaknesses of their opponents. A good serve helps (the player who delivers it) to control the play and put pressure on their competition from the start. The shot dictates the flow of the competition and influences players' positions on the court. Thus, the pickleball service is a powerful tool that allows players to set up their game plan and exploit strategic advantages. It also helps them lay the groundwork for each point.

To execute the service, the server stands within the service box, holding the ball below their waist. Using an underhand motion, the server must contact the ball below waist level. The ball must clear the net diagonally and land within the opponent's service court. After the serve, both teams must let the ball to bounce once before returning it. Faults, contact like serving out of bounds or hitting the net, lead to point penalties.

A "let" serve occurs if the ball clips the net but remains in the correct service court, granting the server another attempt. Just like the serve's significance in pickleball, a leader's initial actions in a project or team effort set the tone and trajectory, underscoring the pivotal role of inspiration, communication, and a positive tone in influencing the course of their team's endeavors.

The Skills Required to Hit a Pickleball Serve

Executing a successful pickleball serve requires a blend of technical skill, focus, and strategic thinking. Here are the key skills necessary to execute a pickleball serve:

Ball Control - The ability to control the ball's trajectory and spin during the serve is essential for placing the ball in the opponent's service court.

Grip and Swing - A proper grip and a smooth, controlled underhand swing are crucial for generating the right amount of power and accuracy in the serve.

Placement - Skillful placement involves choosing where to land the ball in the opponent's service court to create an advantageous position for the server's team.

Spin Variation - Being able to put spin on the ball, such as topspin or backspin, adds an element of unpredictability and can make it challenging for opponents to return the serve.

Timing - Timing the contact with the ball correctly is vital for a consistent and effective serve. This ensures the ball clears the net and lands in the desired location.

Footwork - Proper footwork helps maintain balance and generate power during the serve, contributing to a more controlled and accurate shot.

Focus and Concentration - Maintaining focus and concentration while executing the serve helps reduce errors and ensures that the serve is well-placed.

Composure - Staying composed under pressure is essential to delivering a confident and accurate serve, especially in high-stakes situations.

Adaptability -Servers need to adapt to different court conditions, opponents' positions, and their team's strategy to execute a serve that aligns with the overall game plan.

Communication - Effective communication between doubles partners is crucial to ensure it align them with the serving strategy, target area, and intended spin.

Rhythm and Pacing - Establishing a consistent rhythm and pacing in the serve routine can help servers maintain a steady flow and avoid becoming predictable to opponents.

Game Awareness - Being aware of the game's context, including the score and opponent's strengths and weaknesses, informs the server's strategy and shot selection.

Game Strategy - Tailoring the serve strategy to exploit opponent's vulnerabilities or disrupt their game plan contributes to the server's success.

Similar to how these skills contribute to a successful pickleball serve, they also have parallels in leadership. Leaders need to exhibit control, focus, adaptability, and strategic thinking in their decisions and actions. Just as a well-executed serve can set the tone for a rally, effective leadership serves as the foundation for inspiring and guiding teams toward success..

How The Skills Learned From The Pickleball Serve Can Help Leaders Increase Their Influence

The skills you refine from executing the serve in pickleball hold valuable lessons for effective leadership. Just as the serve starts the game, leaders' actions set the stage for their team's journey and performance. Here's how the skills learned from serving can apply to leadership.

Ball Control -Just as controlling the ball's trajectory is essential in serving, leaders need to control their communication and actions to convey their intentions.

Grip and Swing - Leaders should have a firm grip on their responsibilities and navigate challenges with a smooth and calculated approach.

Placement - Similar to placing the ball, leaders need to allocate resources, assign tasks, and delegate responsibilities to the right individuals to optimize team performance.

Spin Variation - Just as varying spin adds unpredictability to the serve, leaders can infuse creativity and innovation into their approach, keeping their team engaged and adaptable.

Timing - Leaders must time their decisions and actions to align with the team's goals and ensure they seize opportunities.

Footwork - Maintaining balanced footwork symbolizes a leader's ability to manage their workload, juggle priorities, and stay grounded amidst various tasks.

Focus and Concentration - Leaders need to maintain focus amid distractions, concentrating on critical tasks and providing clear direction to their team.

Composure - Demonstrating composure during challenging situations fosters a calm and confident environment, reassuring team members and enhancing their trust in leadership.

Adaptability - Just as servers adapt to changing conditions, leaders need to adjust their strategies based on shifting market dynamics, emerging trends, and unexpected obstacles.

Communication - Effective communication between leaders and team members enhances collaboration, ensures alignment, and promotes a shared understanding of goals.

Rhythm and Pacing - Establishing a steady pace in leadership, marked by consistent expectations and routines, helps maintain a productive flow and keeps the team motivated.

Game Awareness - Leaders with keen awareness of market trends, customer needs, and their team's strengths can make informed decisions that lead to success.

Game Strategy - Similar to strategic serving, leaders need to craft and implement strategies that leverage their team's strengths and capitalize on opportunities.

Applying these skills in leadership fosters an environment where individuals are empowered to perform at their best. Leaders who embody these qualities can inspire and guide their teams, navigating challenges with precision, adaptability, and a focus on achieving the desired outcomes. Just as a well-executed serve can set the tone for a successful rally, effective leadership serves as the cornerstone for driving teams toward excellence and triumph.

How Sam, The Pickleball Coach, Inspired His Team to Greatness by Applying The Skills he Learned From The Pickleball Serve

Sam's journey from a novice pickleball player to an inspiring coach showcased how the skills he learned from the pickleball serve translated into his leadership style. Introduced to pickleball by a friend, Sam approached the game with curiosity and enthusiasm. As he developed his skills on the court, he realized that the dynamics of serving held valuable lessons that extended beyond the game itself.

Sam's experience serving in pickleball paralleled his realization that, in leadership, a strong start can set the tone for success. As he began coaching pickleball teams, he took to heart the lessons he learned from serving—precision, communication, and strategic thinking. Just as he placed his serves to gain an edge in the game, he positioned his coaching approach to inspire and empower his teams.

Drawing on the skill of communication, Sam used his coaching platform to create a positive tone that resonated with his players. He understood that the first interactions with his team were akin to serving in a game—his initial messages and actions could inspire trust, enthusiasm, and a sense of purpose. Sam's clear communication of goals, expectations, and his belief in the team's capabilities set the stage for collaborative efforts.

Like timing the contact with the ball during a serve, Sam timed his coaching interventions to maximize their impact. He recognized that offering guidance and support at the right moments boosted his players' confidence and decision-making. Much like his well-executed serves cleared the net, his coaching interactions empowered his players to overcome challenges and reach their potential.

Sam's commitment to adaptability, as he adjusted his serves to varying game conditions, mirrored his flexibility in leadership. He tailored his coaching strategies to cater to individual player strengths and team dynamics, fostering an environment where each member felt valued and motivated.

Just as the skill of setting the pace marked a successful serve, Sam's leadership pace embodied consistent engagement, motivation, and support for his players. His steady rhythm kept the team focused and energized, much like the momentum he created with his pickleball serves.

Sam's journey from a pickleball novice to a transformative coach showcased the remarkable convergence of pickleball skills and leadership prowess. The lessons learned from executing a successful serve—communication, precision, timing, and adaptability—formed the bedrock of his coaching philosophy. Sam's story illuminated how the serve of influence, much like the pickleball serve, was the cornerstone of his ability to inspire his teams to achieve greatness and embrace the spirit of teamwork.

Final Thoughts

The serve in pickleball, much like leadership, is more than just starting a rally. In the same way a well-executed serve sets a positive tone for a rally, effective leadership creates motivation, commitment, and success. Effective leaders realize that their actions and words can serve as a powerful force. They understand that their mere presence can elevate the mood of their team members, just like a motivating serve energizes a match. These leaders are not just managers; they are motivators, role models, and mentors. They inspire by example, showcasing dedication, determination, and a relentless pursuit of excellence.

The concept of the serve extends to the art of setting the stage, both in pickleball and leadership. Leaders who set a positive tone create an environment where innovation flourishes, embrace challenges as opportunities, and encourage individuals to push their boundaries.. Teams transcend being just a group of individuals in such a setting.

Leaders who have mastered "The Serve of Influence" possess the ability to inspire not only during moments of triumph but also in times of adversity. They provide unwavering support, much like a consistent serve that keeps the rally alive. They maintain their composure under pressure, reassuring their team members and enhancing trust in leadership.

In addition, effective leaders realize their influence goes beyond just themselves. They empower team members to become leaders in their own right, promoting a culture of leadership at all levels of the organization. In this way, leadership becomes a collective effort, with each member serving their unique role in advancing the team's mission.

"The Serve of Influence" concludes that leadership is beyond authority as it involves inspiration, empowerment, and creating a platform for greatness. Just as a well-placed serve can lead to an exhilarating rally, effective leadership can lead to remarkable achievements. It is a journey that requires continuous self-improvement, a commitment to fostering growth in others, and an unwavering belief in the potential of a team. So, as you step onto the court of leadership, remember the power of your serve, and use it to inspire your team to reach new heights of greatness.

CHAPTER THREE

THE SECOND SHOT

HOW TO REACT WHEN THINGS ARE THROWN AT YOU

I n pickleball, and in life, there are times when you have no choice but to react. In this chapter, we explore the parallels between the strategic return of a pickleball serve and the responses leaders make when unexpected situations arise. Just as the returner adjusts their technique to the serve's spin and direction, leaders must navigate unanticipated events with resilience, adaptability, and a strategic mindset. Join us as we unravel the lessons of the pickleball serve return and apply them to the realm of leadership, where the ability to respond skillfully paves the way for triumph over adversity.

What is The Pickle Serve Return (The Second Shot)?

The pickleball "second shot" is the response to the opponent's serve. This action signifies the shift from serving to strategic positioning, setting the tone for the rally.

When a player receives the serve, they typically aim to regain control and set up their team for an advantageous position with their second shot. To do this, they must strategically place the ball in the opponent's court while obeying the no-volley zone rule near the net.

To perform the second shot, a combination of skills is necessary, including anticipation, positioning, and precision. Athletes must rapidly decide which shot to use, evaluate their position on the court, and analyze the trajectory and spin of the serve. Players may choose to use a controlled drop shot, deep drive, or well-angled shot, depending on the serve to gain an advantage.

The second shot's significance lies in its role as a stepping stone towards either offensive or defensive strategy. A well-placed second shot can set up the server's team for an offensive position at the net, putting pressure on the opponents and dictating the direction of the rally. Conversely, a defensive second shot can create more distance between the players, allowing the receiving team to establish their stance and counter the opponents' attack.

In the broader context of the game, the second shot showcases players' adaptability and strategic thinking. Their ability to assess the situation, make swift decisions, and execute shots that complement their overall game plan is essential. By skillfully handling the second shot, players can create openings, seize control of the court, and ultimately gain the upper hand in the rally, emphasizing the integral role of this shot in the intricate tapestry of pickleball strategy.

Making this shot requires a combination of technical finesse, astute anticipatory skills, and strategic knowledge. This begins with the returner anticipating the serve, which involves reading the spin and trajectory before their opponents execute the shot. By having foresight, the player can position themselves optimally on the court and intercept the ball. Agile footwork is vital for the player to get to the correct spot. By doing this, they can create power and maintain balance. The proper technique is to contact the ball in front of your body. For best results, aim to do this at waist height or a little lower. This ensures maximum control and accuracy. The returner uses a shortened, but controlled swing. He lifts the paddle from low to high and completes the motion with a quick follow-through.

The Skills Required To Hit The Second Shot

The second shot in pickleball plays a significant role in determining the momentum of the rally. A well-calculated return, that factors in the opponent's serve, enables players to position themselves within the point and plan their tactics accordingly. The second shot requires the following key skills:

Anticipation and Reaction -Like reading the serve, the returner must anticipate the incoming ball's speed, spin, and placement, enabling them to react promptly.

Footwork - Agile footwork helps the returner get to the ball in time, set up properly, and generate power for an effective shot.

Adaptability - Responding to varying serve types requires adaptability. Returners adjust their approach to handle serves with different spins and speeds.

Decision-Making Under Pressure - Making quick decisions on shot placement and type while under pressure is a skill similar to decision-making in leadership roles.

Strategic Shot Placement - Returners should direct the ball strategically to create opportunities or exploit opponents' weaknesses.

Communication (Doubles Play) - Effective communication between partners ensures proper positioning, reducing the risk of confusion and missed opportunities.

Precision and Control - Returners need to execute their shot with precision and control to place the ball accurately and avoid giving opponents an advantage.

Adaptive Strategy - Adjusting the return strategy based on the serve's characteristics reflects the ability to adapt strategies to changing circumstances, a critical leadership skill.

Composure - Staying composed during the return, even under pressure, influences shot quality and maintains a focused demeanor.

Team Collaboration (Doubles Play) - Returners in doubles play must collaborate with their partner to determine who will take the return and who will continue the rally.

Mastering the serve return in pickleball requires honing these skills to respond effectively when the ball is "hit" at the returner. Translating these skills to leadership means being adept at anticipating challenges, adapting to unexpected situations, making informed decisions under pressure, and collaborating effectively with the team to achieve successful outcomes.

How The Skills Learned From The Second Shot Apply to Leadership

The skills gained from mastering the pickleball serve return hold profound relevance when applied to leadership roles. These skills, honed through the art of responding effectively to incoming challenges, have direct parallels in the realm of guiding teams and organizations. Here's how you can apply the skills you learned from the pickleball serve return to leadership:

Anticipation and Adaptability -Just as the returner anticipates the serve's trajectory, leaders must anticipate industry trends, market shifts, and potential challenges. This foresight enables leaders to adapt their strategies proactively and position their teams advantageously.

Decision-Making Under Pressure -The split-second decisions made during a serve return mirror the rapid choices leaders must make under pressure. The ability to analyze information swiftly and make informed decisions is vital in navigating critical leadership moments.

Strategic Thinking - Similar to strategically placing the return to exploit opponents' weaknesses, leaders strategically allocate resources, delegate tasks, and position team members to leverage strengths and achieve organizational goals.

Effective Communication - The communication between doubles partners during a return is akin to the need for clear and open communication in leadership. Leaders who communicate goals, expectations, and changes foster transparency and alignment within their teams.

Collaboration and Teamwork - Just as doubles players collaborate in executing a return, leaders must collaborate with their teams to achieve collective objectives. A collaborative approach encourages diverse perspectives and fosters innovation.

Precision and Control - Precision in executing the return corresponds to the precision leaders need in their decision-making and actions. Leaders who are detail-oriented and maintain a high level of accuracy can guide their teams more effectively.

Adaptive Strategy - Adjusting the return strategy based on varying serve attributes reflects leaders' ability to pivot strategies based on changing market dynamics and evolving circumstances.

Composure and Resilience - The composure displayed by a returner facing challenges mirrors the resilience leaders must exhibit when encountering setbacks. Maintaining a composed demeanor fosters confidence and stability among team members.

Team Cohesion - Effective teamwork in doubles play, where partners complement each other's strengths, aligns with the collaborative dynamics leaders establish within their teams to ensure everyone works cohesively toward common goals.

Quick Thinking and Problem-Solving - Like the rapid decision-making in a return, leaders need to address unexpected problems promptly and come up with innovative solutions.

Agile Decision-Making - The adaptability required to handle different serve types is akin to leaders' ability to adjust their strategies and approaches based on changing situations.

The skills learned from the pickleball second shot can be integrated into leadership practices to help individuals overcome challenges, promote teamwork, and achieve successful outcomes. Applying these skills in leadership creates a dynamic, adaptive, and impactful leadership journey, just as a well-executed return sets the stage for a positive rally.

How Vince, The Engineer, Used His Second Shot Skills to React to Problems

His coworkers recognized Vince as a detail-oriented engineer who tackled projects with precision and creativity. One day, while having lunch with another engineer, his colleague mentioned a cool sport called pickleball. After discovering a game that contains elements of tennis, ping-pong, and badminton, Vince decided to give it a try.

He vividly remembered his first day on the pickleball court, unsure of what was to come. With a borrowed paddle in hand, he stepped onto the court and observed the experienced players taking part in quick exchanges. He experienced both excitement and nervousness while waiting to return his first serve in position.

Vince's initial attempts to hit the ball were a combination of misses and awkward hits. But he was determined to improve. He observed how players used their second shot to strategically position the ball and establish the game's rhythm. Every match allowed him to improve his ability to read the spin and trajectory of the serves directed to him, ultimately leading to his skill in executing well-placed second shots.

Vince discovered that in pickleball, the second shot was more than just a strategic move, it was a mentality. The second shot required qualities such as quick decision-making, adaptability, and precision, which he shared with his role as a leader in his engineering team.

While in charge of an important project, Vince faced an unforeseen challenge. The project's timeline was at risk because of delays faced by a key supplier. His pickleball experiences inspired him to ponder the split-second decisions he made during the second shot. Like reading his opponent's serve, he strategically assessed the project situation and planned a well-calibrated response.

Using the skills he honed on the pickleball court, Vince quickly collaborated with his team to identify alternative solutions and adapt their approach. The countless second shots he took helped him refine his ability to adapt under pressure, which proved invaluable. Vince's quick and strategic response overcame the challenge and ensured project success, much like a well-placed second shot in a rally.

The way Vince went from an amateur pickleball player to leveraging his second shot abilities in engineering leadership showcased how sports and professional life can interact in a dynamic way. His improved quick decision-making, adaptability, and strategic thinking from pickleball translated into better leadership skills, proving that growth in one area can benefit another.

Final Thoughts

As we conclude our exploration of the second shot in pickleball and its relevance to leadership, we are reminded of how both areas are constantly changing. The second shot in a pickleball rally and in leadership is crucial for reacting to opportunities with agility and precision. Pickleball players adapt their strategy on the fly by reacting quickly to their opponent's return. In the same way, leaders must confidently and adaptively navigate the ever-changing business landscape, responding to unexpected challenges and opportunities.

The second shot underscores the importance of preparation and positioning. Just as a pickleball player must be in the right place at the right time, leaders need to have a strategic vision and a well-prepared team. This foresight allows them to seize opportunities effectively when they arise, much like a well-placed second shot that sets up a winning point. The concept of the second shot teaches us about timing and execution. Leaders, like pickleball players, need to gauge the right moment to act decisively. Whether it's capitalizing on a market trend or making a critical decision for their team, effective timing can be the difference between success and missed opportunities.

In conclusion, the second shot is a metaphor for seizing opportunities in leadership. It reminds us that leaders must be agile, adaptable, and forward-thinking. They must expect the unexpected and react with precision and determination. Just as a well-executed second shot can turn the tide of a pickleball rally, the second shot in leadership can lead to game-changing outcomes. So, as you embark on your leadership journey, keep the lessons of the second shot in mind, and be ready to react to opportunities with skill and strategy.

CHAPTER FOUR

THE THIRD SHOT DROP

GETTING INTO POSITION

P ickleball's "third shot" is an important part of the game. It combines finesse with tactical ingenuity. This pivotal shot requires players to have a delicate touch and precision as well as a thorough understanding of the court dynamics. The "third shot" transition demonstrates the nuanced decisions required for effective leadership, while simultaneously changing the tempo of the game. Leaders have to navigate complexity, selecting the best approach to lead their teams towards success, much like the third shot-drop, which delicately maneuvers the net, and strategically positions the players on the court. This chapter examines the art and technique of the third shot, its execution and necessary skills. It also explores the connections between pickleball, leadership and the third shot.

What is The Third Shot Drop?

The third shot drop is a fundamental move in pickleball that's used to regain control of the rally after serving and returning. It involves executing a soft and precise shot that lands just beyond the net, often in the opponent's "kitchen" or no-volley zone. A strategic advantage can be gained by players who aim for a gentle arc and a controlled landing, as opponents will be compelled to move forward to engage with the ball while staying at the baseline.

A delicate touch and deep understanding of timing and placement are essential for executing an effective third shot drop. When the serve and return are finished, the player moves towards the kitchen, preparing for a more controlled phase. Clearing the net with ease, they guide the ball with a soft touch and shortened backswing. Ideally, the ball will descend softly and land just beyond the net, inviting opponents to make their move while remaining in the no-volley zone.

The third shot drop is used by players for different strategic purposes. The shot enables the player and their partner to approach the net, gaining an advantageous position to dominate the pace of the rally. Opponents find it challenging to execute aggressive attacks due to the soft landing of the ball, giving the player and their partner an opportunity to take control and start their own offensive moves. The strategic use of the third shot drop can help in gaining positional advantage, disrupting the opponent's rhythm, and setting the stage for a more controlled and collaborative rally phase.

The Skills Required To Hit The Third Shot Drop

Mastering the Third Shot Drop demands a blend of finesse, precision, and strategic insight. This delicate stroke is a fusion of skillful execution and keen court awareness, contributing to its crucial role in the pickleball game. Here are the key skills required to hit the Third Shot Drop:

Touch and Feel -The Third Shot Drop hinges on a player's touch and feel for the ball. Achieving the perfect amount of power and spin to guide the ball over the net and into the no-volley zone requires a sensitive touch and a deep understanding of ball dynamics.

Spin Control - Applying the right spin to the ball imparts the soft landing necessary for the Third Shot Drop. The backspin applied helps the ball lose speed quickly after the bounce, making it a challenging target for opponents to attack.

Height and Arc - Achieving the ideal height and arc over the net is crucial. Too much height risks giving opponents an opportunity to attack, while too little could result in hitting the net. A balance between height and arc ensures the ball clears the net comfortably and lands within the no-volley zone.

Placement - The Third Shot Drop is not just about lofting the ball over the net; it's about placing it accurately. Targeting the landing zone near the opponent's baseline while avoiding their net player is a skill that requires precision and strategic thinking.

Anticipation - Anticipating opponents' positions and movements is essential. Understanding where opponents are likely to be after the return allows players to choose the right angle and placement for the Third Shot Drop, making it challenging for opponents to counter effectively.

Soft Touch - A gentle touch is essential to prevent the ball from bouncing too far upon landing. The Third Shot Drop's objective is to keep the ball within the no-volley zone, necessitating a soft touch that minimizes its bounce after the first contact with the court.

Adaptability - Adapting the Third Shot Drop to various situations enhances its effectiveness. Whether it's countering an aggressive return or capitalizing on opponents' positioning, the ability to adjust the shot based on the ever-changing dynamics of the game is paramount.

Consistency - Consistency is key to incorporating the Third Shot Drop into one's repertoire. Developing the muscle memory to consistently execute this shot ensures players can rely on it in high-stakes situations.

Court Awareness - Recognizing the court's layout and anticipating how the shot will interact with its surfaces and angles is essential. An acute awareness of the court helps players adjust their execution based on the game's context.

The mastery of these skills elevates the Third Shot Drop from a mere stroke to a strategic tool that can shift the dynamics of the game. These skills mirror the qualities needed in effective leadership – precision, anticipation, adaptability, and a nuanced understanding of the environment. Just as hitting the Third Shot Drop sets the stage for tactical maneuvers in pickleball, honing these skills can place leaders in a strategic position to guide their teams toward success.

How The Skills Learned "The Third Shot Drop" Can Help Leaders "Get into Position"

The skills that players acquire while mastering the Third Shot Drop in pickleball are more than just strokes; they are potent tools that leaders can wield to strategically position themselves for success. Much like executing the Third Shot Drop requires finesse and precision, leaders need to finesse their strategies and position themselves effectively. Here's how the skills learned from the Third Shot Drop can seamlessly translate into leadership:

Anticipate and Plan - Just as players anticipate their opponents' moves for the Third Shot Drop, leaders must anticipate challenges and market shifts. By proactively planning for potential disruptions, leaders can position their teams to adapt and thrive in changing circumstances.

Precision in Decision-Making - The precision needed for the Third Shot Drop parallels the accuracy leaders must apply in decision-making. Leaders who make well-calculated decisions can steer their teams toward the right course of action, positioning them for success.

Adaptability - Much like the Third Shot Drop is adapted to opponents' positions, leaders must adapt their strategies to evolving situations. Agile leaders can pivot their approaches when faced with unforeseen challenges, positioning their teams for effective responses.

Strategic Placement - Just as players strategically position the Third Shot Drop, leaders must position their resources, talent, and efforts to achieve optimal results. Proper resource allocation and task delegation can create an environment conducive to achieving objectives.

Communication - Effective communication is essential for both pickleball and leadership. Just as players communicate through shot placement, leaders must communicate clearly with their teams, positioning everyone to work collaboratively and cohesively.

Consistency - Consistently executing the Third Shot Drop is vital, and the same applies to leadership. Consistent leadership builds trust and predictability, positioning leaders as reliable guides for their teams.

Strategic Thinking - Strategic thinking is integral to the Third Shot Drop and to leadership as well. Leaders who think strategically can envision long-term goals, align actions, and position their teams for sustainable success.

Environmental Awareness - In the same way players consider court layout, leaders must be aware of their organizational environment. Understanding market trends and internal dynamics empowers leaders to make informed decisions and position their teams optimally.

Soft Touch and Emotional Intelligence - Just as a soft touch is required for the Third Shot Drop, emotional intelligence is essential for leaders. Leaders who exhibit emotional intelligence can navigate interpersonal dynamics, positioning themselves as effective guides for their teams.

By infusing these skills learned from the Third Shot Drop into their leadership approach, leaders can navigate the complexities of their roles with finesse. Through anticipating, adapting, and making strategic decisions, leaders position themselves to steer their teams through challenges and capitalize on opportunities, ultimately paving the way for success.

How John, The Sales Executive, Used The Skills Learned From "The Third Shot Drop" to Get Into Position

John, a dynamic sales executive, is renowned for his exceptional ability to read clients and cleverly navigate intricate negotiations. John's enthusiasm for pickleball flourished during a team-building event that took place outside the corporate world. He never imagined that his pickleball abilities would become so important in his role as a sales leader.

John's interest in pickleball began with his first game, where he picked up a paddle and played with colleagues. He was drawn in by the game's mix of strategy, finesse, and anticipation. He discovered a remarkable connection between the complexities of pickleball and the skill of effective sales management as he honed his abilities.

A pivotal day brought John to a very important client meeting. The high-stakes deal on the table called for a delicate touch because of the client's changing needs. By drawing inspiration from his pickleball experiences, John saw that the Third Shot Drop skills he had cultivated could apply to his sales approach.

As John contemplated the situation, he recognized that just as the Third Shot Drop demanded precision and anticipation, his client interaction required the same meticulous planning. He meticulously analyzed the client's evolving needs and anticipated potential questions and concerns that might arise during the meeting. Much like the finesse he applied to the Third Shot Drop, John adapted his approach to communicate empathy and understanding, aligning his strategy with the client's shifting requirements.

The backspin he had perfected in the Third Shot Drop played a role in John's communication as well. He employed a delicate touch, ensuring that his solution landed gently with the client. This prevented any unnecessary bounce-back that could hinder productive dialogue.

Throughout the meeting, John showcased his adaptability—a skill he had meticulously refined on the pickleball court. Like a seasoned player assessing opponents' positions, John pivoted his approach based on the client's cues. His capacity to switch strategies mid-conversation exemplified how the skills learned from pickleball could be seamlessly transferred into his leadership role.

As John maneuvered through the meeting, his strategic placement of solutions mirrored the thoughtfulness with which he placed the Third Shot Drop on the pickleball court. He seamlessly balanced his suggestions, demonstrating an in-depth understanding of the client's needs while fostering an environment of trust and collaboration.

Much like a Third Shot Drop sets the stage for subsequent plays in pickleball, John's adept positioning during the meeting paved the way for productive follow-up interactions. The client was not only impressed by John's precision and adaptability but also by his ability to seamlessly navigate their evolving requirements.

John's journey from a team-building pickleball match to harnessing Third Shot Drop skills in the sales arena exemplified the unexpected synergy between sports and professional acumen. His capacity to anticipate, adapt, and execute strategic decisions allowed him to consistently position himself as a sales leader who not only secured deals but also cultivated enduring client relationships.

Final Thoughts

As we conclude our exploration of the second shot in pickleball and its relevance to leadership, we are reminded of how both areas are constantly changing. The second shot in a pickleball rally and in leadership is crucial for reacting to opportunities with agility and precision. Pickleball players adapt their strategy on the fly by reacting quickly to their opponent's return. In the same way, leaders must confidently and adaptively navigate the ever-changing business landscape, responding to unexpected challenges and opportunities.

The second shot underscores the importance of preparation and positioning. Just as a pickleball player must be in the right place at the right time, leaders need to have a strategic vision and a well-prepared team. This foresight allows them to seize opportunities effectively when they arise, much like a well-placed second shot that sets up a winning point.

The concept of the second shot teaches us about timing and execution. Leaders, like pickleball players, need to gauge the right moment to act decisively. Whether it's capitalizing on a market trend or making a critical decision for their team, effective timing can be the difference between success and missed opportunities.

In conclusion, the second shot is a metaphor for seizing opportunities in leadership. It reminds us that leaders must be agile, adaptable, and forward-thinking. They must expect the unexpected and react with precision and determination. Just as a well-executed second shot can turn the tide of a pickleball rally, the second shot in leadership can lead to game-changing outcomes. So, as you embark on your leadership journey, keep the lessons of the second shot in mind, and be ready to react to opportunities with skill and strategy.

CHAPTER FIVE

THE THIRD SHOT DRIVE

KEEPING YOUR COMPETITION OFF BALANCE

The "third shot drive" is a pickleball shot that offers players an alternative to the commonly used third shot drop. Unlike the soft and gentle approach of the drop, the drive involves hitting the ball with more power and speed, aiming to send it deeper into the opponent's court. This shot is executed as a way to counter opponents who might be anticipating a soft drop, catching them off guard and maintaining an offensive stance.

What is The Third Shot Drive?

The "third shot drive" in pickleball contrasts with the more common third shot drop by offering players an alternative strategy to maintain an offensive advantage. Executed with a controlled burst of power and speed, the third shot drive involves hitting the ball deeper into the opponent's court, catching them off guard and maintaining an assertive stance. To execute the shot, a player positions themselves near the baseline after the serve and return, generating power through a compact but controlled backswing, and striking the ball with precision to send it on a slight upward trajectory. The objective is to place the ball deep into the opponent's court close to the baseline, creating a challenge for them to react swiftly and return effectively.

The third shot drive is employed strategically when a player wishes to maintain an offensive position after the serve and return, rather than transitioning to a defensive posture as with the third shot drop. This shot is particularly effective against opponents who may anticipate a softer shot, such as the drop, enabling players to surprise their opponents with the change in strategy. By sending the ball deep into the opponent's court, the player aims to capitalize on the element of surprise, maintain their momentum, and create opportunities for future shots. The third shot drive showcases the versatility of pickleball tactics, allowing players to keep their opponents on their toes, dictate the pace of the game, and ultimately seize control of the court.

The Skills Required to Hit a Third Shot Drive

There are a number of skill required to hit an effective third shot drop, including:

Power Control - Executing the third shot drive demands a balance between power and control. Players need to generate enough force to send the ball deep while avoiding excessive power that could lead to an out-of-bounds shot.

Timing - Timing is crucial, as players must hit the ball while it's still low to the ground. This requires a well-timed swing to catch the ball at the optimal moment.

Placement - Just as with any pickleball shot, placement is critical. The ability to send the ball close to the baseline while avoiding the net and sideline contributes to the shot's effectiveness.

The Surprise Factor - The third shot drive aims to catch opponents off guard. Players need to disguise their intentions well to prevent opponents from anticipating the shot too early.

Adaptability - Players must assess the situation quickly and decide whether to execute a drop or a drive based on opponents' positioning and readiness.

The third shot drive serves several strategic purposes including:

Maintaining Offense - While the drop shot focuses on transitioning to the net, the drive allows players to maintain an offensive stance and keep opponents on their heels.

Surprising Opponents - The change from a softer drop to a more forceful drive can catch opponents by surprise, disrupting their anticipation and response.

Creating Opportunities - The deeper placement of the drive can create opportunities for subsequent shots, as opponents might be forced to hit an upward shot that can be attacked at the net.

Strategic Variation - Having both the drop and the drive in one's repertoire offers players a strategic advantage, as opponents cannot predict the shot type consistently.

The third shot drive exemplifies the versatility of pickleball tactics, showcasing that players have multiple tools at their disposal to navigate different situations. By developing the skills required for the drive, players can keep opponents guessing, maintain control of the game, and set themselves up for future successes.

How The Skills Learned From The Third Shot Drive Can Help Leaders Keep Their Competition Off Balance

The skills honed through mastering the third shot drive in pickleball offer a valuable toolkit that extends seamlessly into leadership roles. The shot requires adaptability and quick decision-making on the court, similar to the qualities required for leaders facing dynamic business environments. Leaders aligning with their organization's goals and responding to market changes must make strategic decision-making, such as choosing a drop or a drive. And, the shot demands the same level of timing and precision as well-timed actions and precise execution in leadership pursuits.

The third shot drive's inherent surprise element showcases innovative thinking in leadership. This creates paths for collective success for leaders who can strategically position their teams, just like the shot creates opportunities for other shots. The art of executing the third shot drive involves balancing power and control, and leaders must navigate this balance by balancing authority and collaboration.

The leaders need to respond to emerging challenges and seize fleeting opportunities is mirrored in the rapid decision-making and adaptability required to execute the third shot drive. By learning skills such as quick assessment, calculated action, strategic placement, and power modulation on the court, individuals can become empowered leaders capable of making informed choices, adapting strategies, and driving impactful outcomes.

Ultimately, the skills learned from the third shot drive transform into a leadership toolkit, equipping leaders with the ability to navigate uncertainty, make timely decisions, foster innovation, and strategically position their teams for success. Let's inspect how each of these skills can help leaders.

Adaptability and Quick Decision-Making - Just as players must decide between a drop or drive in a split second, leaders often face rapidly changing circumstances that demand quick adaptability and effective decision-making to guide their teams through uncertainty.

Strategic Decision-Making - Similar to selecting the right shot, leaders must strategically choose actions that align with their organization's goals and respond to market dynamics, making decisions that position their teams for success.

Timing and Precision - The timing and precision required for the shot translate to leaders' need for well-timed actions and precise execution in project management, resource allocation, and seizing opportunities.

Innovative Thinking and Surprise Tactics - Like surprising opponents with the change from a drop to a drive, leaders who employ innovative thinking can disrupt the status quo and foster a culture of creative problem-solving within their teams.

Opportunity Creation - Just as the third shot drive sets up opportunities for subsequent actions, leaders who strategically position their teams can create pathways for success, leveraging their resources and strengths effectively.

Balancing Power and Control - The skill of balancing power and control while executing the shot mirrors leaders' challenge to assert their authority while fostering a collaborative environment where team members feel empowered to contribute their best.

Rapid Decision-Making and Adaptability:** The quick decision-making and adaptability practiced on the court align with leaders' need to swiftly assess situations, respond to challenges, and pivot strategies when necessary.

Strategic Placement and Impact - Placing the ball effectively in the opponent's court is akin to leaders positioning their teams for maximum impact, orchestrating efforts to align with organizational goals and create meaningful outcomes.

The skills gleaned from mastering the third shot drive provide leaders with a dynamic skill set that enables them to navigate ambiguity, make well-timed decisions, drive innovation, and strategically guide their teams to success.

How Ray, The Business Development Professional, Used The Skills Learned From Pickleball To Keep His Competition off Balance

Meet "Ray," a driven business development professional whose journey to mastering the third shot drive in pickleball transformed not only his approach on the court but also his competitive edge in the business world. Ray's introduction to pickleball started with a casual invitation from a colleague. Curiosity piqued, he decided to give it a try and found himself captivated by the sport's strategic nuances and physical demands.

As Ray immersed himself in pickleball, he discovered the third shot drive—a technique that soon captured his attention. Its blend of power, surprise, and strategic intent resonated deeply with his approach to his business ventures. Inspired by the lessons from the court, Ray began to see the potential application of the third shot drive's principles in his profession.

Drawing parallels between the assertive nature of the third shot drive and his business strategies, Ray realized that maintaining an offensive stance in the business world was equally crucial. Embracing the element of surprise that the shot offered, he incorporated innovative and unanticipated approaches into his communication with potential clients and partners. This fresh perspective allowed him to stand out and create a lasting impression in an increasingly competitive market.

Much like sending a well-placed ball deep into his opponent's court, Ray found ways to penetrate the market and create opportunities that positioned him advantageously. By embracing the skill set learned through executing the third shot drive, he showcased his agility in responding to market shifts and effectively leveraging new avenues for business growth.

Ray's journey from a curious pickleball newcomer to a business development innovator illustrates the seamless integration of skills acquired from the court to the professional realm. His story is a testament to how seemingly unrelated experiences can converge to enhance strategic thinking, resilience, and adaptability—qualities that propel both pickleball players and business professionals to excel in their chosen fields.

Final Thoughts

As we wrap up our exploration of the third shot drive in pickleball and its intriguing implications for leadership, we gain deeper insights into the interplay between power and precision, both on the court and in the world of leadership.

Just as the third shot drive demands a balance between power and accuracy, leaders must strike a similar equilibrium in their decision-making and actions. This chapter underscored the importance of knowing when to assert power and when to wield precision to achieve desired outcomes, be it in a pickleball rally or in the boardroom.

By adopting a measured approach, they can have an influence on situations and make important decisions, similar to a well-executed third shot drive that keeps opponents on edge. Leaders, like skilled pickleball players, must harness their resources effectively and apply power judiciously. This measured approach allows them to influence situations and make impactful decisions, much like a well-executed third shot drive that keeps opponents on their toes.

The concept of the third shot drive also highlights the significance of precision and control. Leaders need to execute their plans with precision, ensuring that each decision aligns with their strategic goals. The ability to maintain accuracy amid dynamic circumstances is a hallmark of effective leadership, similar to the precise placement of a third shot drive.

In conclusion, the third shot drive serves as a metaphor for leadership that combines power and precision. It reminds us that leaders must master the art of applying strength when needed, while maintaining control and precision in their actions. Just as a well-executed third shot drive can shift the momentum in a pickleball rally, leadership that balances power and precision can drive teams and organizations toward success. As you embark on your leadership journey, keep the lessons of the third shot drive in mind, and be prepared to wield both strength and accuracy to achieve your goals.

Chapter Six

THE DINK

The Precision of a Visionary Strategist

The dink shot in pickleball is a masterclass in finesse and precision. It involves delicately tapping the ball over the net with minimal power, causing it to drop just inches from the net on the opponent's side. Executed with a soft touch and careful control, the dink shot aims to exploit gaps in the opponent's positioning, forcing them to react to the slow-paced shot. The dink requires impeccable timing, as players must adjust their stance and paddle angle to execute the shot with utmost accuracy. This shot is a testament to the art of subtlety and controlled decision-making, as players anticipate their opponents' moves and strategically position themselves to achieve a well-placed shot. As we dissect the mechanics of the dink shot, we uncover its strategic nuances and draw parallels to the finesse required in making crucial decisions within the realm of leadership.

What is the "Dink" Shot?

The dink shot is an exercise in precision and control. To perform this delicate maneuver, players need to adopt a soft touch and finesse that contrasts with the power-driven shots commonly seen on the court. As the ball approaches, players adjust their stance and paddle angle, ensuring that the paddle face is slightly angled upwards. The key lies in making contact with the ball gently, creating a smooth and controlled motion that guides the ball over the net. The dink shot's objective is not to overpower opponents, but rather to exploit openings and force them to react under the pressure of a well-placed shot.

The Skills Required to Hit The Dink Shot

Perfecting the dink requires an innate understanding of timing, anticipation, and spatial awareness, as players craft shots that gracefully clear the net and land just inches from the sideline. Executing it requires a number of skills that contribute to finesse and precision. These skills include:

Controlled Touch - Players need to possess a delicate touch to gently tap the ball, allowing it to clear the net with minimal force.

Paddle Angle - Properly angling the paddle is crucial for directing the ball's trajectory accurately over the net and onto the opponent's side.

Timing - Timing is paramount for successful execution. Players must judge the ball's speed, height, and bounce to make contact at the optimal moment.

Anticipation - Anticipating the opponent's positioning and movement is essential to identify open spaces where the dink shot can be strategically placed.

Footwork - Positioning is key. Players need agile footwork to adjust their stance and move into the appropriate position to execute the shot effectively.

Controlled Power - While the dink shot requires minimal power, players must exert just enough force to clear the net and place the ball close to it.

Decision-Making - Making quick decisions about when and where to execute the dink shot involves strategic thinking and adapting to changing circumstances.

Deception - Concealing one's intentions until the last moment adds an element of surprise to the dink shot, making it harder for opponents to anticipate and react.

Variation - Varying the angle, height, and placement of dink shots keeps opponents guessing and prevents them from predicting the shot's trajectory.

Consistency -Consistently executing accurate dink shots requires practice and mastery of the technique to ensure reliable results.

How The Skills Learned From The Dink Apply to Leadership

The skills necessary for successful dink shots in pickleball, including controlled touch, paddle angle, timing, anticipation, footwork, controlled power, decision-making, deception, variation, and consistency, bear a striking resemblance to the qualities crucial for effective leadership. Let's explore how these abilities can effortlessly transform into leadership skills.

Controlled Touch - Just as players require a delicate touch to guide the ball, leaders need to navigate sensitive situations with finesse. Addressing sensitive matters and conflicts with a gentle approach enhances relationships and maintains harmony within the team.

Paddle Angle - Similar to angling the paddle for precise ball placement, leaders must direct their communication and decisions accurately. Crafting messages tailored to resonate with the audience ensures that directives and feedback are effectively conveyed.

Timing - Timing is not only crucial in dink shots but also in leadership. Leaders must time their decisions to align with the team's goals and seize opportunities, ensuring that actions yield maximum impact.

Anticipation - Leaders who anticipate market trends, shifts in industry dynamics, and their team's needs can strategize effectively and make informed decisions that position their organization advantageously.

Footwork - Just as players adjust their stance for optimal shot execution, leaders must position themselves strategically. Agile leadership requires adapting to change swiftly, aligning with the organization's goals, and responding to dynamic challenges.

Controlled Power - Like players use controlled power to clear the net, leaders must exert the right amount of influence to drive initiatives. Overexertion can be counterproductive, just as underutilizing power may lead to missed opportunities.

Decision-Making - The split-second choices players make when executing a dink shot are akin to the quick decisions leaders face daily. Swift yet thoughtful decisions are vital for navigating challenges and seize opportunities.

Deception - Keeping intentions under wraps until the right moment can be a leadership asset. By strategically withholding information, leaders can unveil initiatives at opportune times, generating a sense of anticipation and curiosity.

Variation -Varying leadership approaches, much like altering dink shot angles, prevents predictability. Leaders who diversify their strategies create engaging environments and adapt to changing team dynamics.

Consistency - The practice and mastery required for consistent dink shots align with leadership consistency. Reliable leadership inspires trust and fosters an environment where team members can depend on their leader's guidance.

The skills honed through the finesse of executing dink shots remarkably parallel the attributes that define effective leadership. By embracing these skills, leaders can tactfully navigate challenges, make informed decisions, and guide their teams to success with grace and precision.

How Scott, The Cannabis Dispensary Manager, Became a Visionary Strategist

Scott's journey from corporate executive to a more effective leader began in a rather unexpected place — the pickleball court. As the manager of a bustling cannabis dispensary, his role demanded not only business acumen but also the finesse to navigate the unique challenges of the industry. Little did he know that his introduction to pickleball would offer invaluable insights into leadership dynamics.

Curious about the game, Scott started playing pickleball during his free time. Initially drawn to the sport's camaraderie and recreational appeal, he quickly realized its strategic parallels with his managerial responsibilities. The "dink" shot, in particular, caught his attention. Scott recognized the shot's subtle power, as it required precision and timing to outmaneuver opponents.

Inspired by the finesse required in the dink shot, Scott began to apply similar principles to his leadership role. He understood that the cannabis industry, like pickleball, demanded a deft touch. The regulatory landscape was evolving rapidly, and customers' needs were diverse and ever-changing. Scott saw the opportunity to approach leadership with a calculated finesse that mirrored the strategic placement of a well-executed dink shot.

Just as the dink shot disrupts opponents' expectations, Scott's newfound leadership finesse disrupted conventional approaches. He fine-tuned his decision-making, opting for calculated, nuanced moves rather than reactive choices. This strategic approach created a ripple effect in his dispensary's operations. By anticipating shifts in customer preferences and regulatory changes, Scott positioned his dispensary to not only survive but thrive in the competitive market.

A pivotal moment came when Scott's dispensary faced a critical inventory shortage due to supply chain disruptions. Instead of panicking, he channeled the dink shot's strategic philosophy. With precision, he collaborated with suppliers, streamlined internal processes, and introduced alternative products to maintain customer satisfaction. His ability to control the game's pace and position his dispensary for long-term success mirrored the mastery of the dink shot.

Over time, Scott's reputation as a strategic leader grew within the cannabis industry. His approach — combining adaptability, foresight, and calculated decisions — set him apart as a visionary who had embraced the lessons of pickleball. As he continued honing his dinking skills on the court, his leadership prowess became even more evident at work.

Scott's journey from a corporate executive to an impactful leader underscored the unexpected intersections between sportsmanship and business acumen. The finesse he learned from pickleball profoundly transformed his approach, elevating his ability to navigate challenges, make well-timed decisions, and strategically position his dispensary for enduring success. Just as the dink shot can alter the course of a pickleball game, Scott's finesse-driven leadership significantly reshaped the trajectory of his organization.

Final Thoughts

Our investigation of the dink shot in pickleball and its connections to leadership is ending. Now, let's focus on the importance of precision, patience, and tactical finesse, which are indispensable in both pickleball and leadership. The dink shot teaches a valuable lesson in precision through its emphasis on soft touches and calculated placement. A well-executed dink and leadership have one thing in common: the need for precise control over actions, decisions, and communication. This precision allows leaders to navigate complex situations with grace and purpose, much like the careful placement of a dink shot.

Leadership also requires patience, which is another important aspect of the dink. It's crucial for leaders to recognize that powerful responses or immediate action aren't needed in every situation. Effective leaders know the importance of waiting for the right moment, like a player setting up a dink. Like a player patiently setting up a dink, effective leaders understand the power of waiting for the right moment to make their move. This patience allows them to make thoughtful decisions that align with long-term objectives. Waiting for the right moment to make their move is a skill effective leaders possess, like a player setting up a dink.

The dink shot also underscores the value of tactical finesse. Leaders, like skilled pickleball players executing dinks, must employ strategic subtlety and craftiness in their approaches. The ability to outmaneuver challenges with finesse rather than force is a hallmark of effective leadership, similar to the artful execution of a dink shot.

To sum up, the dink shot is a symbol of leadership that highlights accuracy, composure, and strategic skill. It reminds us that effective leaders can achieve remarkable results by exercising control, waiting for the right opportunities, and employing strategic subtlety. Just as a well-executed dink can outwit opponents on the pickleball court, leadership that embodies these qualities can navigate complex challenges with elegance and success.

CHAPTER SEVEN

THE ERNIE

PROACTIVE, INITIATIVE AND INNOVATION IN LEADERSHIP

S ome pickleball shots go beyond the norm and impress both opponents and spectators. One such shot is the "Ernie," a daring maneuver that requires both audacity and precision. But the Ernie is more than just a shot; it's a testament to the power of proactivity and initiative in pursuing innovation. This section of the book explores Ernie Leadership and how the audacious Ernie shot can be a beacon for leaders seeking to spearhead innovative efforts. The art of quick reflexes, bold moves, and the element of surprise are revealed as we examine settings such as the pickleball court and the boardroom. Learn how the Ernie shot and visionary leadership work together to drive innovation and embrace change with unwavering confidence.

What is The Ernie Shot?

The Ernie shot in pickleball transcends conventional play with its boldness and audacity. To perform the Ernie shot, a player near the sideline sprints to the opposite side of the court and hits the ball while it's airborne, prior to crossing the net. By taking this high-risk, high-reward shot, opponents are caught off guard and forced to react quickly, disrupting their positioning. To make the shot, you need perfect timing, quick reflexes, and a readiness to explore the unknown. It is an embodiment of innovation and proactivity, showcasing the player's 's determination to seize the moment and create an unexpected advantage. Let's analyze some of the critical elements in executing the Ernie.

Positioning - The player strategically positions themselves outside the court, close to the sideline, anticipating that the opponent's return shot will be directed cross-court.

Anticipation - As the opponent hits the ball, the player predicts the trajectory and timing of the return shot. Anticipation is key; the player must read the opponent's body language and paddle angle to predict where the ball will be.

Quick Reflexes - With split-second reflexes, the player lunges toward the ball and executes a swift, angled shot while keeping one foot out of the court. This is what sets the Ernie shot apart — the player hits the ball while partially outside the boundaries of the court.

Placement - The Ernie shot is typically aimed down the line, hugging the sideline and aiming to clear the net and land in the opponent's court, preferably beyond their reach.

Surprise Element - The success of the Ernie shot often relies on its unexpected nature. The opponent may not anticipate the player hitting the ball from outside the court, giving the shot a higher chance of success.

Executing the Ernie shot successfully requires a combination of daring initiative, quick reflexes, and a deep understanding of the opponent's playing style. It's a high-risk, high-reward move that can shift the momentum of the game if performed accurately. Players who master the Ernie shot use it selectively and strategically, often when the opponent's positioning and shot selection make it a viable option.

How The Skills Learned From The Ernie Shot Apply to Leadership

Similar to how the Ernie shot demands seizing a moment of opportunity with boldness, leaders who embody the spirit of the Ernie shot embrace proactivity and quick decision-making in the business world. Just as the shot requires a blend of anticipation and quick reflexes, leaders who adopt the Ernie approach navigate through challenges by anticipating trends, taking calculated risks, and seizing unexpected opportunities to drive innovation and success.

Business leaders must also use positioning, anticipation, quick reflexes, placement, and the element of surprise to achieve success, drawing parallels between these qualities in both the context of pickleball and leadership. Here are some examples:

Positioning - In pickleball, players position themselves strategically to be ready for their opponents' shots, ensuring they are well-placed to react effectively. In leadership, positioning involves situating oneself and the team in a way that maximizes the potential for success. Leaders need to position resources, teams, and strategies to navigate challenges and seize opportunities.

Anticipation - In pickleball, players must anticipate the trajectory of the ball based on their opponents' movements and shot selection, enabling them to prepare for their next move. In leadership, anticipation entails foreseeing trends, shifts in the market, and potential obstacles. Leaders anticipate changes to make informed decisions that keep their organizations ahead of the curve.

Quick Reflexes - In pickleball, quick reflexes are crucial for reacting to fast-paced shots and unexpected changes in the game, enabling players to make accurate returns. In leadership, quick reflexes involve adapting swiftly to changing circumstances and making timely decisions. Leaders who respond promptly to challenges and opportunities can steer their teams effectively.

Placement - In pickleball, players carefully place their shots to create advantageous positions on the court, exploiting opponents' weaknesses and setting up for follow-up shots. In leadership, placement involves making well-thought-out decisions that position an organization for success. Leaders strategically allocate resources, talent, and initiatives to optimize outcomes.

Element of Surprise - In pickleball, players use surprise shots like the Ernie shot to catch opponents off guard, increasing the likelihood of scoring points. In leadership, the element of surprise can lead to innovation and competitive advantage. Leaders who introduce unexpected strategies, products, or approaches disrupt the norm and set their organizations apart.

Both in pickleball and leadership, positioning and anticipation enable individuals to be better prepared for what's ahead. This increases their chances of success. Quick reflexes are essential for adapting to changing circumstances and taking advantage of fleeting opportunities, whether on the court or in business.

While the placement of shots in pickleball affects a specific point in a game, placement decisions in leadership often have broader and longer-lasting implications for an organization's trajectory. In pickleball, the element of surprise can lead to short-term gains by catching opponents off guard. In leadership, surprise can lead to lasting innovation and market disruption, contributing to long-term success.

The qualities that lead to success in both pickleball and leadership are closely intertwined. The ability to position oneself, anticipate, react quickly, strategically place actions, and introduce elements of surprise can lead to exceptional outcomes, whether on the pickleball court or in the complex world of business leadership.

How Yung, The Software Developer, Embraced Bold Moves And Quick Reflexes to Spearhead Groundbreaking Initiatives

Yung's transformation from a software developer to a proficient leader was an inspiring journey that began on the pickleball court and was driven by the embodiment of the audacious "Ernie" shot. As a diligent programmer, Yung's expertise in coding was unparalleled, but he soon discovered that the lessons from an unexpected source could elevate his leadership skills to new heights.

Yung's journey into pickleball was a result of a casual invitation from a friend. Intrigued by the unique blend of athleticism and strategy, Yung embraced the opportunity to try something new. The "Ernie" shot captured his attention immediately. The daring move, executed from beyond the court boundaries, symbolized a leap of faith and a willingness to seize opportunities in unconventional ways.

Just as the Ernie shot required Yung to position himself creatively outside the confines of the court, he recognized the importance of positioning himself in the tech industry. He understood that thinking outside the box was a key component of leadership. With this insight, Yung approached his role with a fresh perspective, positioning himself and his team to explore uncharted territories and disrupt industry norms.

Anticipation was Yung's next skill acquired from the Ernie shot. In pickleball, he honed the ability to predict his opponent's moves, translating this to the business arena where he anticipated market trends and the ever-evolving needs of his customers. This anticipation empowered him to make agile decisions, much like the quick reflexes needed to perform the Ernie shot on the court.

As Yung executed the Ernie shot with precision, he learned that placement was paramount. Translating this lesson to his leadership role, he strategically positioned his team's talents and resources to achieve optimal outcomes. Yung's decisions mirrored the strategic placement of the Ernie shot, aiming to take calculated risks that pushed boundaries and propelled his team forward.

The element of surprise inherent in the Ernie shot became a driving force for Yung's leadership style. Embracing unexpected strategies, he introduced innovative approaches that set his team apart from competitors. Yung understood that, much like the Ernie shot caught opponents off guard, surprise in the business world could lead to breakthroughs that reshaped industries.

Yung's metamorphosis from software developer to visionary leader was complete. His journey on the pickleball court, where he learned to embrace the spirit of the Ernie shot, had a profound impact on his approach to leadership. The once reserved programmer had become an audacious leader who positioned himself creatively, anticipated market shifts, executed decisions with precision, and infused his strategies with an element of surprise.

Through his story, Yung demonstrated how skills acquired from an unexpected source can have a remarkable impact on leadership. Just as the Ernie shot defies convention to achieve success, Yung's leadership style defied norms to drive innovation, ultimately positioning his team for sustained success.

Final Thoughts

By being audacious and proactive, the Ernie shot shows us how crucial it is to take initiative. Players who execute an Ernie in pickleball leap daringly and swing rapidly. In the same way, leaders must understand the worth of seizing opportunities and making courageous moves when the moment is appropriate. The Ernie shot exemplifies how proactive leadership leads to innovation and progress.

Another important aspect emphasized by the Ernie is innovation. The shot is an inventive modification of classic pickleball methods that highlights the influence of innovation in game-changing ways. Leadership requires innovation to be equally essential. Encouraging innovation in teams can lead to a fertile environment for groundbreaking ideas to grow, just like the innovative spirit that inspired the Ernie shot.

The Ernie shot is an example of how bold moves can be transformative. An Ernie shot can affect a game's trajectory, just like bold leadership decisions can transform an organization's course. Those who lead fearlessly, take calculated risks, and think outside the box are often at the forefront of positive change.

In closing, the Ernie shot is a symbol of leadership that encompasses initiative, creativity, and the transformative power of daring actions. For effective leadership, seizing opportunities, fostering innovation, and making daring decisions are crucial. Leadership that embraces these qualities can take teams or organizations to new heights, much like a successful Ernie shot can redefine a point in pickleball. Remember the Ernie shot as you begin your leadership journey and strive for innovation, proactivity, and boldness in your pursuit of excellence.

CHAPTER EIGHT

MASTERING THE KITCHEN ZONE

THE ART OF ESTABLISHING BOUNDARIES

In pickleball, the "kitchen" or "no volley zone" is an important area on the court. It stretches 7 feet on both sides of the net. Its intention is to create a fair balance between offense and defense by prohibiting players from volleying near the net. The key to dominating the kitchen is not only following rules, but also mastering the art of establishing leadership boundaries.

This chapter discusses the mechanics of the kitchen zone and its effect on the game, revealing its significant implications for effective leadership. Get ready to explore strategic positioning, ethical decision-making, and creating a dynamic playing field that empowers individuals and teams to thrive within established boundaries. Learn how the kitchen zone concept helps leaders cultivate success through thoughtful limitations.

What is The Kitchen?

Within the kitchen, players are prohibited from hitting the ball out of the air, and they must wait for the ball to bounce before entering and making a shot. The foot fault rule applies, meaning that both feet must remain outside the kitchen while hitting the ball to avoid a fault. While volleys can be executed outside the kitchen, this designated area encourages players to adopt a more controlled and strategic approach to their shots. As a strategic hotspot, the kitchen adds depth to pickleball gameplay, urging players to master shot placement, anticipate bounces, and carefully navigate their positioning to achieve success. Mastering the kitchen requires that players understand and adhere to the following rules:

The No Volley Zone - In the kitchen, players are not allowed to hit the ball out of the air, i.e., they cannot volley the ball while their feet are within the no volley zone. A volley is a shot where the player strikes the ball before it bounces on the ground.

The Foot Fault Rule - To execute a legal shot within the kitchen, players must ensure that both feet are positioned outside the kitchen before making contact with the ball. If a player's foot touches any part of the kitchen (including the line), it is considered a fault.

After the Bounce - Players can enter the kitchen and hit the ball only after the ball has bounced once on the ground. This rule is in place to prevent players from approaching the net and hitting aggressive shots before the ball has a chance to bounce.

Volleys Outside The Kitchen -Players can hit volleys from outside the kitchen, whether behind the baseline or near the sidelines. However, they must be careful not to step into the kitchen area while hitting the ball.

Strategic Importance - The kitchen's proximity to the net makes it a strategic area for both offensive and defensive play. Skilled players use shots that arc over the net and land in the kitchen, creating challenging returns for opponents. Additionally, players can strategically position themselves near the kitchen to react quickly to opponents' shots.

How The Rules of The Kitchen in Pickleball Apply to Leadership

The rules of the kitchen in pickleball establish a framework for fair play and strategic engagement. They also offer a captivating metaphor for effective leadership. The concept of the kitchen zone resonates deeply with the necessity for leaders to establish boundaries and adhere to ethical principles. Much like players must avoid foot faults by respecting the kitchen's boundaries, leaders must maintain a strong ethical foundation in their decision-making.

The rule that mandates players wait for the ball to bounce within the kitchen zone before engaging parallels the importance of leaders taking a deliberate pause before making decisions, allowing for informed and considered choices. As players craft precise shots to navigate the no volley zone, leaders must carefully position their strategies, initiatives, and resources within the organizational landscape.

The rules of the kitchen in pickleball serve as a poignant reminder that effective leadership requires strategic positioning, ethical considerations, and a balanced approach to decision-making within the boundaries of the larger context.

Concepts like the "no volley zone," "foot fault rule," "after the bounce," "volleys outside the kitchen," and strategic innovation offer valuable insights into leadership behaviors and approaches. Let's take a look at each of these more closely.

No Volley Zone -Just as the no volley zone prevents players from hitting volleys near the net, leaders should establish boundaries for their decision-making. Some decisions require a pause for reflection rather than immediate action. Leaders can set a "no volley zone" for significant choices, giving themselves time to evaluate potential outcomes and consider alternatives before making a final call.

Foot Fault Rule - The foot fault rule emphasizes the importance of maintaining a solid foundation. In leadership, this translates to remaining grounded in ethical principles and values. Leaders who stray from their foundational values risk making decisions that are out of alignment with their organization's mission and can potentially lead to negative consequences.

After the Bounce - The "after the bounce" principle teaches leaders to observe, assess, and learn from their actions before proceeding.

By reflecting on past decisions and their outcomes, leaders can gain valuable insights that inform future choices. This concept encourages leaders to adopt a continuous improvement mindset and make adjustments based on experience.

Volleys Outside the Kitchen - Leaders can draw inspiration from the concept of volleys outside the kitchen by considering the broader context when making decisions. Just as players position themselves strategically to execute volleys effectively, leaders should position themselves to view the larger organizational landscape. Making decisions based on a holistic understanding of the situation ensures more impactful outcomes.

Strategic Innovation - Strategic innovation in pickleball involves anticipating opponents' moves and proactively adjusting strategies. Leaders can apply this concept by fostering a culture of innovation within their teams. Encouraging employees to anticipate market shifts and industry trends, and empowering them to propose innovative solutions, can lead to a more agile and forward-thinking organization.

Incorporating these pickleball concepts into leadership behaviors encourages a thoughtful, strategic, and ethical approach to decision-making. By establishing boundaries, staying grounded in values, reflecting on past actions, considering the bigger picture, and fostering innovation, leaders can guide their teams toward success while navigating the complexities of the ever-changing business landscape.

How Brent, a Small Business Owner, Created a Harmonious Workplace by Setting The Right Boundaries And Promoting Teamwork

Brent's journey from a small business owner to a skilled leader was an unexpected one, ignited by his introduction to the game of pickleball and his mastery of the "kitchen zone." As the owner of a local cafe, Brent's aspiration to enhance his leadership skills led him to a remarkable transformation that paralleled the principles of the pickleball court.

Brent's pickleball journey began when he stumbled upon a community event promoting the sport. Intrigued by the fusion of athleticism and strategy, he decided to give it a shot. The "kitchen zone" or "no volley zone" particularly captured his attention. As he navigated this restricted area near the net, he discovered that its principles could be applied to the challenges he faced as a business owner.

Much like how players must exercise caution in the kitchen to avoid foot faults, Brent recognized the importance of maintaining a solid foundation in his business endeavors. Just as stepping into the kitchen area results in a fault, straying from his business's core values could lead to unfavorable outcomes. With this insight, Brent reaffirmed his commitment to the values that had shaped his cafe's identity, ensuring that every decision aligned with these guiding principles.

The concept of "after the bounce" resonated deeply with Brent. As he witnessed the ball's bounce on the pickleball court before making a shot, he realized the value of observing before acting. Translating this to his leadership role, Brent began to step back and evaluate the outcomes of his decisions before charging forward. This practice empowered him to identify patterns, fine-tune strategies, and adapt to changes, fostering a culture of continuous improvement within his cafe.

Brent's grasp of the kitchen zone's strategic importance allowed him to position himself thoughtfully in the ever-evolving business landscape. Just as players position themselves strategically to execute well-placed shots, Brent positioned his cafe to cater to changing customer preferences and market trends. By focusing on precision and calculated moves, he successfully differentiated his cafe from competitors, much like a player's well-placed shot clears the net and lands in the kitchen.

Moreover, Brent's journey embodied the spirit of strategic innovation. By translating the game's principles to his business, he encouraged his team to anticipate shifts in the market and propose innovative solutions. Just as players anticipate opponents' moves, Brent's team embraced a proactive approach that allowed them to pivot and adapt swiftly to new challenges and opportunities.

Brent's transformation from a small business owner to an adept leader was a testament to the power of learning from unexpected sources. The lessons of the pickleball kitchen zone cultivated a leadership style grounded in core values, focused on continuous improvement, and driven by strategic innovation. His cafe thrived as a result, serving as a living example of how the principles from the pickleball court could be skillfully applied to the art of leadership.

Final Thoughts

The kitchen area is a powerful metaphor for leadership, with its meticulous rules and the delicate balance between offense and defense. Leaders must set ethical boundaries to guide their team's decisions, similar to how boundaries create a fair playing field in pickleball. The boundaries serve as a compass, guiding the team towards ethical choices and responsible conduct.

Strategic positioning is key to success in both the kitchen and leadership. To succeed, leaders need to make informed decisions, adapt to evolving circumstances, and empower their teams. In the same way that players move around the kitchen, leaders position themselves strategically to navigate their industries or organizations.

The kitchen zone concept underscores the importance of ethical decision-making in leadership. Leaders are required to make ethical decisions that are in accordance with the values of their organization and themselves. Upholding integrity and accountability boundaries is how ethical leaders establish trust and credibility in their teams, much like how players honor kitchen boundaries for a fair game.

The kitchen zone in pickleball is a reminder of the significance of ethical boundaries and strategic positioning in leadership. It underscores the importance of ethical decision-making and the profound influence of boundaries on team dynamics. Just as a well-mastered kitchen ensures fairness in pickleball, leadership that embraces these principles creates an environment of trust, responsibility, and ethical conduct. As you continue your leadership journey, remember the lessons of the kitchen and use them as a compass to guide your team toward success within the boundaries of ethics and strategy.

CHAPTER NINE

THE LOB

A METAPHOR FOR VISIONARY LEADERSHIP

The "lob shot" is more than a strategic maneuver—it's a metaphor for visionary leadership that spans beyond the immediate horizon. In this chapter, we look at the intricacies of the lob shot, a high-arcing shot that propels the ball over opponents' heads, landing deep in their court. As we explore the mechanics of the lob shot, we unveil the resonances it holds with the world of leadership, where long-term vision and strategic positioning are essential. Just as the lob shot requires foresight and precision to create opportunities for success, leadership demands a comparable ability to anticipate future trends, inspire teams, and cultivate a vision that extends beyond the present moment. Embark on this journey with us as we delve into the parallels between the lob shot and the power of visionary leadership, uncovering how the ability to strategically position resources, navigate challenges, and propel one's team toward long-term success mirrors the artistry of executing a perfectly placed lob shot on the pickleball court.

What is The Lob Shot?

The lob shot involves gently lifting the ball high into the air, creating an arcing trajectory over the net and landing deep within the opponent's court. This tactic proves especially effective when adversaries are near the net, compelling them to quickly retreat towards the backcourt to retrieve the ball. To execute the lob shot, players adjust their grip and angle it upward for paddle control. The timing is crucial as players anticipate the ball's trajectory and initiate the loft by making contact underneath. A well-calculated arc and placement are crucial to the shot's success, with the goal of landing the ball near the opponent's baseline. By frequently surprising opponents who expect aggressive shots, the lob shot disturbs the game's tempo and creates opportunities for advantageous follow-ups. Executing this shot however, requires players to master a number of skills. a few of them are listed below.

Positioning - The lob shot is often used when opponents are positioned near the net, anticipating aggressive shots. This positioning allows the lobber to exploit the empty space in the back of the court.

Grip and Angle - The player uses a grip that provides control over the paddle's angle. The paddle face is tilted slightly upward to generate the necessary lift for the lob.

Timing -Timing is crucial. As the ball approaches, the player adjusts their body positioning and paddle angle to accommodate the desired trajectory of the lob.

Contact - The player makes contact with the ball underneath, slightly lifting it into the air. The angle of contact determines the height and distance the ball will travel.

Arc and Placement - The player aims to create a high, looping arc over the net. The goal is to land the ball deep in the opponent's court, ideally near the baseline, making it challenging for opponents to return effectively.

Element of Surprise - The effectiveness of the lob shot often relies on the element of surprise. Since opponents are often positioned near the net, they may not anticipate a high-arcing shot and may struggle to respond quickly enough.

Follow-Through - A smooth follow-through motion ensures that the ball's trajectory remains consistent, allowing it to achieve the desired arc.

The purpose of the lob shot goes beyond just scoring points. It has the ability to reset the game's tempo, allow for strategic repositioning, and force opponents to adjust their tactics. Players use the lob shot to shift the momentum strategically, control the court, and generate opportunities for follow-up shots.

To execute a lob shot, one needs finesse, control, and a deep understanding of opponents' positioning. Successful execution of the shot demands precision in timing, angle, and follow-through. Skillful players use the lob shot to keep their opponents guessing and gain an advantage in the game.

How The Skills Learned From The Lob Shot Can Apply to Leadership

Mastering the lob shot in pickleball can translate into leadership skills and offer insights into strategic acumen and long-term vision. Visionary leaders possess the ability to anticipate market trends, industry shifts, and emerging opportunities, guiding their teams towards sustainable success, just as executing the lob shot demands foresight regarding the ball's trajectory.

Just as players position the ball strategically to gain a competitive edge, leaders position their teams, resources, and initiatives to take advantage of market dynamics, giving their organizations a competitive advantage. The timing and patience needed for a well-placed lob shot resembles the leadership quality of being patient, knowing when to act and when to wait, and avoiding impulsive decisions that could harm long-term goals. In both contexts, effective communication and alignment are paramount. Players communicating with their partners or visionary leaders fostering clear communication and alignment within their teams.

Adapting strategies to changing market conditions can help leaders remain relevant and seize opportunities, much like adjusting the lob shot technique to the ball's trajectory. Players executing the lob shot need to assess the risks and rewards, similar to evaluating risks and rewards when making strategic decisions. Those with a compelling vision have the ability to inspire their teams to overcome challenges and achieve ambitious goals. Visionary leadership requires lob shot skills such as foresight, strategic thinking, and the ability to navigate complex decision-making, to achieve lasting success for organizations. Let's explore how the lob skill and leadership intersect.

Positioning - In leadership, positioning involves strategically aligning resources, teams, and strategies to achieve desired outcomes. Leaders must position themselves as well-informed decision-makers by gathering insights from various sources. Just as players position themselves on the court, leaders need to position their organization within the competitive landscape to make informed decisions that yield positive results.

Grip and Angle - Similar to adjusting the grip and angle for optimal shot execution, leaders need to tailor their approach to different situations. Just as the right grip impacts shot accuracy, choosing the appropriate leadership style and angle to address challenges can lead to more effective outcomes.

Timing - Effective leaders understand the importance of timing in decision-making. Acting too hastily or delaying crucial choices can have significant consequences. Just as timing affects shot success, leaders must recognize the right moment to seize opportunities, address issues, or pivot strategies for maximum impact.

Contact - In leadership, effective communication is the equivalent of making successful contact in pickleball. Leaders need to connect with their team members, stakeholders, and clients to build strong relationships. Just as successful contact propels the ball forward, effective communication drives collaboration, innovation, and overall success.

Arc and Placement - The concept of arc and placement translates to strategic decision-making in leadership. Just as a well-placed shot in pickleball puts the ball out of opponents' reach, leaders strategically position their actions, initiatives, and resources to achieve specific objectives. This involves considering the broader organizational context and aiming for outcomes that create the most value.

Element of Surprise - In leadership, the element of surprise corresponds to innovation and disruption. Just as surprising opponents with unexpected moves can lead to points in pickleball, leaders who introduce innovative strategies, products, or solutions can gain a competitive advantage. The element of surprise encourages creativity, keeps competitors on their toes, and positions the organization for success.

Follow-Through - Leadership requires consistent follow-through to ensure that plans are executed effectively. Just as a smooth follow-through in pickleball impacts the ball's trajectory, a leader's commitment to overseeing projects, tracking progress, and making necessary adjustments ensures that strategies reach their intended destinations. Effective follow-through maintains momentum and prevents efforts from falling short of the mark.

Incorporating these concepts from pickleball into leadership practices underscores the importance of precision, strategy, adaptability, and effective communication. By mastering these parallels, leaders can navigate challenges, anticipate opportunities, and guide their teams toward long-term success.

How Rebecca, The School Counselor, Became a Visionary Leader by Learning How to Lob

Rebecca's journey to becoming a more effective leader was fueled by the sport of pickleball and the lessons she learned from mastering the lob shot. Rebecca's interest in the game's blend of strategy and finesse led an avid player colleague to introduce her to pickleball. She began to play regularly at a nearby community center, where she learned the complexities of the game, particularly the lob shot's tactical finesse.

Rebecca discovered that the lob shot's principles on the pickleball court were applicable to her leadership role. The lob shot and being a school counselor both require her to understand others' movements and emotions. Similar to the lob shot's precise timing, Rebecca understood the significance of timing her interventions and support for students, noticing when they required encouragement, advice, or a listening ear.

Rebecca drew inspiration from the lob shot's long-term focus during a particularly challenging meeting with a student who was struggling academically and emotionally. She didn't look for instant remedies, but instead envisioned the student's journey and devised a comprehensive plan to provide ongoing support. Just as the lob shot aimed to extend the point, the shift in perspective did the same. It occurred to Rebecca that fostering long-term development yielded more results than tackling isolated problems.

Additionally, the lob shot's strategic placement strongly connected with Rebecca's leadership approach. While guiding her students, collaborating with teachers and working with parents, she positioned her interventions strategically to align with individual needs and overarching goals. Similar to how a well-placed lob shot could disrupt opponents' positioning, Rebecca's interventions could positively disrupt negative patterns and create positive change.

Rebecca's change was obvious not just in how she engaged with students, but also in her leadership amongst the school community. As a leader, she elevated her effectiveness by envisioning long-term goals and navigating immediate challenges with tact. By mastering the lob shot, she developed skills like foresight, strategic positioning, and long-term focus, which enabled her to create a more supportive and dynamic educational environment. Playing pickleball and mastering the lob shot gave Rebecca leadership insights that would forever transform her approach and impact as a school counselor and leader.

Final Thoughts

Leadership can be compared to the lob shot because it prioritizes long-term positioning and deliberate elevation. A long-term vision that guides actions and decisions is crucial for leaders, just like a well-executed lob shot helps players reposition strategically. A well-executed lob shot enables players to strategically reposition themselves, just as leaders must have a long-term vision to guide their actions and decisions.The lob shot emphasizes the significance of being adaptable.

The lob shot sheds light on how crucial adaptability is. In pickleball, the lob shot is a strategic response to opponents' aggressive play, showcasing the power of adaptability in the face of adversity. Leaders must possess the skill to adapt to changing circumstances, market dynamics, and unforeseen challenges. Adaptable leaders can navigate uncertainty better by pivoting and adjusting their strategies. Leaders who can pivot and adjust their strategies effectively often find themselves better equipped to navigate uncertainty.

The lob shot underscores the transformative influence of strategic planning. Similar to a well-planned lob shot that throws off opponents, strategic planning in leadership can alter the course of an organization. Lasting success can be laid by leaders who engage in thoughtful, forward-looking planning.eaders who engage in thoughtful, forward-looking planning often lay the groundwork for lasting success.

CHAPTER TEN

POACHING FOR PROGRESS

COLLABORATION AND SUPPORTIVE LEADERSHIP

P oaching is a strategic move that can be applied beyond the pickleball court to represent strong leadership. Like players who poach to intercept shots and surprise opponents, leaders can also use collaboration, proactive support, and timely interventions to drive progress within their teams and organizations. This chapter takes a closer look at poaching's strategic finesse and how it can shape the leadership landscape. Be prepared to witness how the principles of leadership that propel individuals, teams, and organizations towards lasting success align with the dynamic world of pickleball, from fostering open communication to seizing opportunities.

What is Poaching?

The act of "poaching" is used in pickleball to intercept a shot meant for a partner who is positioned closer to the net. The goal is to gain an advantage during a rally by using a tactic that surprises opponents and disrupts their rhythm. Creating confusion and forcing opponents to make rushed shots result from effective poaching.

In order to execute a poach, the player who intends to intercept the shot must cross quickly in front of their partner and take over the shot opportunity. The player predicts the path of the ball and moves to intercept it, hitting it before it reaches their partner. For this strategy to work, partners must have excellent communication and understanding, with the poaching player making sure they don't collide with their partner while keeping them informed of their decision to poach.

Poaching is an effective technique that can add an element of surprise to the game, catching opponents off guard. But, there are also risks involved, as mistimed or mis-communicated poaching attempts can cause errors or missed shots. To successfully poach in advanced pickleball strategy, timing, coordination with the partner, and surprise are crucial elements that make it intriguing and dynamic.

The art of poaching in pickleball requires a combination of strategic awareness, agility, and effective communication to be mastered. Successful poaching requires the following skills:

Communication - Effective poaching hinges on clear communication between partners. Players must signal their intention to poach and ensure their partner is aware and ready for the shift in positioning.

Anticipation - Poaching requires the ability to anticipate opponents' shots and movements. Players need to read the trajectory of the ball and predict where opponents are likely to hit it.

Quick Reflexes - Rapid reactions are crucial for intercepting shots during a poach. Players must be able to change direction swiftly and respond to the ball's movement.

Footwork - Agile footwork enables players to quickly cross over to their partner's side and intercept the shot. Proper footwork minimizes the risk of collisions and ensures a smooth transition.

Timing - Timely execution is essential for successful poaching. Players need to time their movement accurately to intercept the ball at the right moment, without interfering with their partner's shot.

Decision-Making -Poaching involves split-second decisions. Players must decide whether to poach based on factors such as opponents' positioning, shot selection, and court awareness.

Trust - Poaching relies on trust between partners. Players need to trust that their partner will cover their original position while they move to intercept the shot.

Strategic Positioning - Effective poaching requires strategic positioning on the court. Players need to position themselves close enough to their partner to intercept the shot but far enough to avoid hindering their partner's movements.

Coordination - Coordination between partners is crucial for successful poaching. Players need to coordinate their movements to ensure that both players are in sync and poised to react effectively.

Risk Assessment - Players must weigh the risks of poaching against potential rewards. A well-timed poach can lead to a winning shot, but mistimed or poorly executed poaches can leave the court vulnerable.

Adaptability - Being adaptable allows players to adjust their poaching strategy based on opponents' shots, changing circumstances, and the flow of the game.

Confidence - Poaching requires confidence in one's abilities and decisions. Players need to trust their skills and instincts to execute the poach effectively.

Successfully poaching in pickleball reflects a dynamic blend of cognitive awareness, physical agility, and effective teamwork. By mastering these skills, players can disrupt opponents' strategies, seize control of the point, and ultimately contribute to their team's success on the court.

How The Skills Learned From Poaching Apply to Leadership

The skills acquired from mastering the poaching technique are not confined to pickleball alone. In fact, they can have profound implications for the world of leadership, where the ability to intercept opportunities, foster teamwork, and adapt to change are paramount. As we dissect the intricacies of poaching's strategic finesse, prepare to unveil the remarkable parallels between the dynamic maneuvers of the pickleball court and the dynamic challenges faced by leaders in various domains. From communication and anticipation to adaptability and risk management, join us in deciphering how the principles of poaching seamlessly translate to leadership, guiding individuals and teams to navigate uncharted waters with finesse and flourish.

Communication - Just as clear communication is crucial for poaching, leaders who communicate openly and transparently with their teams build trust, facilitate understanding, and ensure everyone is on the same page.

Anticipation - Leaders who anticipate market trends, customer needs, and potential challenges can proactively position their organizations for success, making informed decisions based on foresight.

Quick Reflexes - In a rapidly changing business landscape, leaders with quick reflexes can respond promptly to emerging opportunities or threats, allowing them to adapt and seize advantages swiftly.

Footwork - Agile footwork in leadership involves the ability to pivot and shift strategies when circumstances change. Adapting to new situations and responding to evolving demands is essential for effective leadership.

Timing - Timely decision-making is pivotal for leaders, enabling them to capitalize on opportunities before competitors do, while avoiding rushed or untimely choices that could have negative consequences.

Decision-Making - Leaders must make critical decisions under pressure. Deciding whether to take calculated risks, embrace innovation, or pivot strategies requires strategic thinking akin to the decision to poach.

Trust - In leadership, trust is fundamental. Leaders who cultivate trust among their teams foster a collaborative environment where members rely on one another's expertise and support.

Strategic Positioning - Leaders strategically position their teams and resources to achieve goals, allocating assets effectively and optimizing processes to maximize efficiency.

Coordination - Like partners coordinating their movements during a poach, leaders who foster teamwork and alignment among team members ensure everyone works together cohesively toward shared objectives.

Risk Assessment - Leaders evaluate risks and rewards to make informed choices. Akin to considering whether to poach, leaders assess potential outcomes and decide on actions that offer the best chances for success.

Adaptability - Adaptable leaders are prepared to adjust strategies when circumstances change, embracing new ideas and technologies to remain competitive and relevant in evolving markets.

Confidence - Confidence in decision-making and strategies empowers leaders to guide their teams with conviction, inspiring trust and motivating their teams to reach higher levels of performance.

By drawing parallels between the skills of poaching and leadership, individuals can cultivate a dynamic leadership style that embraces collaboration, anticipates challenges, and seizes opportunities. Just as skilled poaching disrupts opponents' strategies, leaders who embody these skills can disrupt conventional thinking, inspiring innovative solutions and fostering a cohesive, agile, and successful team.

How Irene, The Financial Service Professional, Became a Collaborative And Supportive Leader by Applying The Skills She Learned From Poaching

Irene's love for pickleball inspired a transformation from a financial service professional to a collaborative and supportive leader. Irene began playing pickleball to unwind from her demanding job after being introduced to the game by a friend. She had no idea that her court skills would eventually shape her approach to leadership.

While exploring pickleball, Irene became fascinated by the tactical finesse of poaching. The thought of intercepting shots and working flawlessly with a partner struck a chord with her. Before too long, she saw similarities between poaching on the court and successful financial leadership.

With newly acquired skills from poaching, Irene brought enthusiasm to her leadership role. Communication was the main element. Just like Irene communicated with her pickleball partner during a poach, she promoted open communication within her team. Her team members were able to collaborate effectively, share ideas and express their concerns, creating a cohesive work environment.

Irene's ability to anticipate opponents' moves during a poach translated to her capacity to foresee market trends in the financial industry. She utilized this foresight to position her team strategically, enabling them to offer innovative solutions and stay ahead of competitors.

The skill of quick reflexes, essential for intercepting shots, became invaluable when Irene faced sudden shifts in the market. Her agility in adapting to new circumstances allowed her team to respond promptly to challenges, adjusting strategies to maintain their competitive edge.

One day, during a crucial client meeting, Irene's decision to "poach" by stepping in to address a concern before her colleague had the chance, showcased her supportive leadership style. This act not only demonstrated her commitment to her team's success but also reassured the client of their dedication.

By applying the principles of poaching, Irene nurtured a culture of collaboration, trust, and adaptability within her team. Just as successful poaching required partnership and synchronization, Irene's leadership emphasized teamwork, where everyone's strengths were leveraged to achieve common goals.

Through the seemingly unlikely connection between pickleball and leadership, Irene evolved from a financial service professional to a collaborative and supportive leader. Her newfound approach led to improved team dynamics, enhanced client relationships, and a reputation for innovative problem-solving. With a heart full of enthusiasm and a strategic mindset, Irene continued to draw inspiration from the courtside, using the lessons of poaching to lead with finesse and elevate her team to new heights.

Final Thoughts

The metaphor of poaching, where players intercept shots to support their partner strategically, is a strong representation of leadership. Like poaching, effective leadership relies on teamwork and collaboration within a group or organization. Leaders who prioritize open communication, information sharing, and mutual support set themselves up for success.

In pickleball, poaching exemplifies how a well-timed intervention can turn the tide of a rally in favor of the team. Similarly, in leadership, supportive leaders can step in at the right moment to guide their teams through challenges and steer them toward success. The role of a supportive leader is akin to that of a skilled poacher, intercepting obstacles and facilitating a smoother journey for their team.

This chapter underscored the significance of collaboration and communication. Just as poachers rely on effective communication with their partners, leaders must foster clear and open lines of communication within their teams. Strong communication cultivates trust, encourages the sharing of ideas, and promotes a culture of inclusivity.

Finally, the art of poaching in pickleball reflects the principles of collaboration, teamwork, and supportive leadership. It reminds us that effective leaders must embrace these principles to inspire and guide their teams. Just as a well-timed poach can change the course of a rally, leadership that values collaboration and support can transform organizations and empower teams to achieve remarkable success. As you continue your leadership journey, carry the lessons of poaching with you and let them serve as a reminder of the importance of teamwork, communication, and support in achieving your leadership goals.

CHAPTER ELEVEN

LEADING THE RALLY

PERSEVERANCE THROUGH ADVERSITY

Welcome to the exploration of "Leading the Rally: Perseverance A" Here, we uncover the story of a leader who, like a skilled pickleball player, held the line against obstacles, maintained momentum, and inspired their team to triumph against all odds.

Leaders must demonstrate unrelenting determination in the face of adversity to maintain momentum and accomplish goals, just as players do when they rally to maintain control and eventually seize the point. This chapter illustrates how a leader can inspire their team by fostering resilience, exhibiting unwavering determination in the face of obstacles, and leading by example. Join us on this journey as we explore the inspiring story of resilience, revealing the techniques and mentality that not only maintain momentum but also lead to success in the field of leadership.

What is a Pickleball Rally?

The pickleball rally is a sequence of exchanges between players that occurs after the serve and ends when a point is won or lost. The rally is an exciting and dynamic segment of the game where players use strategy, technique, and teamwork to outsmart opponents and score points. The serve marks the beginning of each rally, in which players must hit the ball across the net and follow certain rules in an effort to land it on the opponent's court.

Successful pickleball rallies require players to execute a variety of skills to maintain control and score points. These skills include:

The Serve - The rally starts with the serving player delivering the ball diagonally across the net to the opponent's court. A well-placed serve can put the receiving team on the defensive from the very beginning.

The Return - The receiving team aims to return the serve, putting the serving team on the defensive. The return should clear the net and land within the boundaries of the opponent's court.

Placement - Throughout the rally, players use strategic shot placement to exploit opponents' weaknesses, create challenging angles, and control the flow of the game.

Volleys -Players often engage in volleys, where they hit the ball before it bounces, using controlled touches to maintain control and maneuver the ball strategically.

Dinks - Dinks involve softly hitting the ball over the net, usually from near the kitchen line, to keep the ball low and close to the net, making it difficult for opponents to attack.

Groundstrokes - Groundstrokes are powerful shots that players execute after the ball bounces. These shots can create opportunities to dictate the pace and direction of the rally.

Footwork - Agile footwork is crucial to getting into the right position for hitting shots and maintaining balance, especially during fast-paced rallies.

Anticipation - Players need to anticipate opponents' shots and movements to react quickly and make well-timed returns.

Communication - Effective communication is vital, especially in doubles play, where players need to coordinate their movements and shot selection.

Adaptability - Adapting to opponents' strategies, adjusting shot selection based on circumstances, and remaining flexible are essential to winning rallies.

Concentration - Maintaining focus and concentration during a rally ensures that players make accurate shots and minimize errors.

A successful pickleball rally causes technical skills, strategic thinking, adaptability, and teamwork. To succeed, players must make quick decisions, execute precise shots, and work cohesively with their partner to maintain control and secure points. Outside of the court, these abilities are valuable leadership qualities that encourage adaptability,

informed decision-making, effective collaboration, and focused perseverance amid challenges.

How The Skills Learned From Leading a Rally Apply to Leadership

Pickleball's rally is the essence of the game - a pulsating exchange
of shots, strategy, and teamwork that concludes with a victorious or
defeated point. Players use their skills to outsmart opponents and
gain a scoring advantage in a high-stakes segment. The skills required
for effective leadership are remarkably mirrored in the dynamics of a
pickleball rally beyond the court lines.

Let's examine the similarities between a pickleball rally and leadership and see how successful rallies can enhance leadership abilities.

The Serve: Initiating Action

As each rally begins, leaders initiate initiatives that propel their
teams forward. A successful leadership "serve" can create the tone and
force competitors to be defensive with a meaningful introduction or
initiative.

The Return: Responding to Challenges

Pickleball receiving teams try to counteract the serve, much like
leaders handle challenges. Composure, creativity, and skillful naviga-
tion are necessary qualities for leaders to handle unexpected situations.

Placement: Strategic Navigation

Shot placement in pickleball exploits opponents' weaknesses. Similarly, leaders use strategic shot placement to capitalize on opportunities, creating angles that lead to successful outcomes.

Volleys: Engaging in Agile Interaction

Leaders interact with agility and make swift and decisive decisions
just like players volleying the ball in a rally.

Dinks: Soft yet Impactful Approach

The term "dink" refers to a subtle yet effective strategy in both pickleball and leadership. The art of leadership involves delicately handling situations to reduce conflict, tension, and promote smoother interactions.

Groundstrokes: Power and Precision

Executed after the ball bounces, groundstrokes are powerful shots. Similarly, leaders make impactful decisions with accuracy and understanding, leading their teams towards success.

Footwork: Agile Maneuvering

Agile footwork is crucial in fast-paced rallies to ensure players are well-positioned for the next shot. Leaders who move quickly can adapt well to change and lead their teams effectively.

Anticipation: Staying Ahead

To deliver well-timed returns, players anticipate opponents' actions. Anticipating market shifts, industry trends, and team dynamics can help leaders make informed decisions for future successes in leadership.

Communication: Synchronizing Efforts

Successful pickleball gameplay requires effective communication. Effective leaders rely on communication, team coordination, vision sharing, and alignment.

Adaptability: Flexibility Amid Change

Adapting strategies mid-rally is key to victory in pickleball, as is adaptability in leadership. Leaders must be open to evolving strategies, adjusting to challenges, and thriving amid dynamic changes.

Concentration: Unwavering Focus

Concentrating during a rally results in precise shots. When leaders concentrate, they make better decisions, minimize errors, and overcome challenges successfully.

The correlation between pickleball rally skills and leadership attributes is apparent, with both relying on quick decisions, precise execution, adaptability, and effective collaboration as their foundations. The tenacity required of leaders when facing intricate challenges is mirrored in the resilience shown in a successful rally.

How Robin, The Church Administrator, Persevered Though Adversity by Applying The Skills She Learned From Leading a Rally in Pickleball

Robin's journey from a church administrator to an unwavering leader was a testament to the lessons she learned on the pickleball court, where leading a rally mirrored her pursuit of success amid adversity. Introduced to pickleball by a friend who saw her potential, Robin initially hesitated to join in. However, her curiosity led her to give it a shot, and little did she know that this decision would eventually shape her leadership approach.

As Robin delved into the world of pickleball, she discovered the intrinsic connection between the game's dynamics and the challenges she faced in her leadership role. Leading a rally, for her, became synonymous with leading a team through moments of adversity. The ebb and flow of a game resonated with the ups and downs encountered in her professional journey.

In the pickleball court, Robin honed the skills required to sustain a rally—adaptability, clear communication, and strategic placement. Applying these skills to her role, she faced challenges head-on, adapting strategies to navigate shifting circumstances, and communicating openly with her team to ensure everyone was on the same page.

During a particularly challenging period, Robin exhibited the resilience she learned from a well-fought rally. Just as she had rallied back
from seemingly losing points on the court, she rallied her team around
a common purpose. She communicated her vision clearly, adapted to
unforeseen obstacles, and exhibited the same precise decision-making
she'd learned from executing shots during a pickleball rally.

Robin's ability to lead a rally was mirrored in her determination
to maintain momentum despite adversity. Instead of succumbing to
setbacks, she embraced them as opportunities for growth. Much like
a player focusing on a critical point during a rally, Robin maintained
her focus on her goals and guided her team through turbulent times.

Robin's story became an inspiration to her colleagues and community, illustrating that leadership is not about avoiding challenges,
but about persevering through them with strength, adaptability, and
unwavering commitment. Drawing from the spirit of a pickleball rally,
Robin proved that leadership's triumphs lie not only in the victories
but in the enduring resolve to lead with integrity, perseverance, and
the unwavering spirit of a true leader.

Final Thoughts

Leading the rally in pickleball is a test of resilience, where players must
endure challenging moments and remain committed to the pursuit
of victory. In leadership, this quality is equally essential. Leaders must
exhibit resilience to navigate the turbulent waters of uncertainty, overcome setbacks, and inspire their teams to persevere.

This chapter on accentuated the significance of adaptability. Just
as players must adjust their strategies during a rally, leaders need to
adapt to changing circumstances, emerging trends, and unexpected

obstacles. Adaptability allows leaders to steer their teams through adversity and seize opportunities.

Moreover, leading the rally emphasizes the importance of sustaining momentum. In both pickleball and leadership, maintaining a positive trajectory is vital for long-term success. Leaders who can foster a culture of continuous improvement, motivation, and shared purpose often find themselves better equipped to lead their teams to greater heights.

Lastly, the concept of leading the rally in pickleball serves as a powerful metaphor for leadership, showcasing the qualities of resilience, adaptability, and the ability to sustain momentum. It reminds us that effective leaders must embody these qualities to inspire their teams through challenges and toward success. Just as a well-led rally can change the dynamics of a game, leadership that embraces these principles can transform teams or organizations and guide them toward enduring success.

CHAPTER TWELVE

THE AROUND THE POLE (ATP) SHOT

EMBRACING LEADERSHIP CREATIVITY

The "Around The Pole" (ATP) shot is a testament to the creative prowess and ingenuity of pickleball players. The audacious shot calls for bending the ball's trajectory around the net post, showcasing technical finesse and an openness to innovation. The ATP shot's spirit reflects the qualities of a leader - envisioning new paths, harnessing unconventional strategies, and inspiring creativity within teams.

This chapter uncovers the magic of the ATP shot and how it mirrors the creative elements of leadership. Much like how players direct the ball around the net post, leaders foster an environment where unconventional ideas can thrive and drive their teams towards uncharted successes. Be ready to explore the intricacies of this shot and find out how fostering innovative ideas can turn leadership into an art form that drives the journey to excellence.

What is The Around The Pole Shot?

The Around The Pole (ATP) shot is a strikingly innovative play in pickleball, designed to bypass the net post and astonish opponents. Imagine this: you're positioned near the baseline, and your opponent has placed the ball so close to the net post that a conventional shot seems impossible. Yet, in a display of creative audacity, you craft an ATP shot – a shot that curves around the net post, teasing gravity and physics alike. With pinpoint accuracy, the ball arcs around the net post, lands gracefully on your opponent's side, and leaves them dumbfounded.

Executed with finesse, the ATP shot is not only a feat of technical skill but also a testament to a player's ability to envision novel trajectories. In this shot, players leverage their mastery of angles, spin, and paddle control to execute the seemingly impossible. Delivering the

Around The Pole (ATP) shot demands a blend of technical prowess, creative vision, and split-second decision-making. Here are the key skills required to master this audacious shot:

Angled Paddle Control - Manipulating the angle of your paddle is crucial to guide the ball around the net post. Players must finesse the paddle's orientation to ensure the ball takes the desired trajectory.

Spin Control - Spin adds finesse to the ATP shot, enabling the ball to curve gracefully. Players need to master topspin or slice, applying just the right amount to achieve the desired effect.

Precision Timing - Timing is everything. To execute the ATP shot successfully, players must make contact with the ball at the perfect moment, allowing it to take the desired path around the net post.

Visual Imagination - Envisioning the ball's trajectory is vital. Players need to mentally map out the shot's arc and predict where the ball will land on the opponent's side.

Adaptability - Court conditions, ball speed, and opponent positioning vary. Adapting to these changing elements while attempting the ATP shot ensures consistent success.

Risk Assessment - The ATP shot involves an element of risk. Players must assess the situation quickly, weighing the potential rewards against the risks before committing to the shot.

Confidence and Creativity - Executing the ATP shot requires a creative spirit and the confidence to attempt something unconventional. Believing in your ability to master this shot is crucial.

Precision Control - A delicate touch is necessary to guide the ball accurately around the net post. Players must control the ball's trajectory and spin to achieve the desired outcome.

Body Positioning - The player's body positioning and movement contribute to the shot's execution. Proper footwork and stance help players generate the necessary power and control.

Concentration - Maintaining focus is essential. Players must concentrate on the shot's mechanics, visualizing the desired outcome, and maintaining composure under pressure.

Practice and Repetition - Mastering the ATP shot requires dedicated practice. Repetition helps players refine their technique, build muscle memory, and enhance shot consistency.

These skills, honed through hours of practice and experimentation, don't merely apply to pickleball. They resonate deeply with leadership, where envisioning innovative solutions, adapting to dynamic circumstances, and executing calculated risks are essential components of success. Just as players craft an ATP shot to astonish opponents, leaders craft creative strategies that inspire and drive their teams to unprecedented heights.

How The Skills Learned From The ATP Apply to Leadership

While the Around The Pole (ATP) shot is a dazzling display of creativity and precision in pickleball, its underlying skills have remarkable parallels in the realm of leadership. Let's investigate how these skills can be leveraged to elevate your leadership game.

Thinking Outside the Box - Just as the ATP shot defies convention, leaders who embrace creativity and unconventional thinking can innovate and devise unique solutions that set their teams apart.

Visionary Decision-Making - The ATP shot requires envisioning a ball's trajectory that seems impossible. In leadership, foresight and the ability to visualize future scenarios allow leaders to make informed decisions that guide their teams toward success.

Calculated Risk-Taking - Executing the ATP shot involves assessing risks and rewards. Similarly, leaders who weigh the potential outcomes and take calculated risks can drive their teams toward break-throughs and game-changing achievements.

Innovation in Problem-Solving - Mastering the ATP shot encourages players to experiment with angles, spins, and timing. Likewise, leaders who foster a culture of innovation inspire their teams to explore new ways of solving challenges and discovering untapped opportunities.

Adaptability and Flexibility - Just as players adjust their shot based on court conditions, leaders who remain adaptable in the face of changing circumstances can pivot their strategies to stay competitive and relevant.

Courageous Leadership - Executing the ATP shot requires confidence to attempt the unexpected. Leaders who exhibit courage can initiate bold initiatives and inspire their teams to pursue ambitious goals.

Strategic Thinking - The ATP shot necessitates meticulous calculation to ensure success. Leaders who strategically plan their moves and anticipate outcomes can steer their teams on a trajectory toward long-term success.

Effective Communication - Communicating intentions to your partner during the ATP shot is crucial. Similarly, leaders who communicate their vision, expectations, and goals with clarity foster alignment within their teams.

Team Collaboration - The ATP shot thrives on teamwork and coordination. Leaders who encourage open collaboration and foster a sense of unity empower their teams to collaborate effectively toward shared goals.

Embracing Failure as a Learning Opportunity - Not every ATP shot will succeed, but failure provides valuable insights. In leadership, embracing failures as learning opportunities can guide improvement and growth.

Empowering Creativity - The ATP shot showcases the power of imagination. Leaders who encourage creativity within their teams unlock innovative solutions and nurture a culture of continuous improvement.

Confidence in Uncertainty - Successfully executing the ATP shot requires confidence even when outcomes are uncertain. In leadership, leaders who radiate confidence inspire their teams and navigate uncertainty with poise.

As you develop your ATP shot skills in pickleball, remember that these skills can serve as a source of inspiration and guidance in your leadership journey. Just as the ATP shot defies expectations on the court, leaders who infuse their leadership style with these skills can shatter norms, foster innovation, and guide their teams toward exceptional achievements.

How Kim, The Entrepreneur, Used the Skills She Learned From The ATP to Become a Creative Leader

Kim, a dynamic entrepreneur, found herself venturing into the world of pickleball, intrigued by its fusion of strategy and athleticism. As she honed her skills on the court, she was particularly captivated by the Around The Pole (ATP) shot—a move that epitomized creativity and innovation. Little did she know that the lessons she gleaned from executing the ATP shot would translate seamlessly into her role as a leader.

Kim's entrepreneurial journey often demanded unconventional solutions and a flair for thinking outside the box. Drawing inspiration from the ATP shot's audacious execution, she began applying similar creative thinking to her business challenges. Just as the ATP shot required her to envision a trajectory that defied norms, Kim started visualizing uncharted pathways for her ventures.

In her leadership role, Kim embraced an innovative mindset, one that questioned the conventional and sought to create new avenues of success. Just as she had strategized the precise spin and placement for the ATP shot, Kim now strategized market entry points and innovative product offerings. The same nimble decision-making that allowed her to execute the ATP shot with split-second timing became an asset in her leadership toolkit, enabling her to navigate swiftly in a fast-paced business environment.

Kim's ATP-shot-inspired skills shone when faced with adversity. She understood that just as the ATP shot required adaptability and adjustment, her leadership needed to be agile in the face of challenges. She leveraged creative problem-solving to address setbacks, turning obstacles into opportunities through imaginative solutions.

Her newfound creativity also extended to fostering a collaborative environment. Just as executing the ATP shot required seamless coordination with her pickleball partner, Kim fostered open communication and teamwork among her employees. She encouraged diverse perspectives, recognizing that collaboration often led to innovative breakthroughs.

Kim's journey from pickleball's ATP shot to leadership creativity became a testament to the power of applying unexpected skills to unconventional settings. Much like crafting the perfect ATP shot, Kim found herself crafting innovative strategies that propelled her ventures forward. With a paddle in hand and a dynamic mindset, Kim embodied the spirit of creative leadership, demonstrating that the lessons learned on the court could serve as a wellspring of innovation in the business world.

Final Thoughts

The ATP shot represents an innovative and creative approach to overcoming obstacles in pickleball. It's a testament to the players' ability to envision unorthodox solutions to challenges and execute them with precision. This spirit of creative problem-solving finds a loud echo in the world of leadership. Effective leaders are often those who encourage creativity and innovation within their teams, allowing novel ideas to flourish and inspiring fresh approaches to age-old problems.

This chapter underscored the importance of daring to be different. Just as pickleball players embrace unorthodox techniques to gain a competitive edge, leaders must break from convention and explore innovative approaches to achieve their goals. Creativity and thinking outside the box often lead to groundbreaking solutions and unparalleled success.

Moreover, the ATP shot highlights the power of seizing the moment. In both pickleball and leadership, recognizing opportunities and taking calculated risks can lead to extraordinary outcomes. Leaders who have the vision to spot opportunities and the courage to act upon them are often the ones who guide their organizations toward innovation and growth.

CHAPTER THIRTEEN

CONCLUSION

As we conclude this remarkable journey through the world of pickleball and leadership, it's abundantly clear that the lessons learned on the court have direct and tangible applications in the realm of leadership. Our exploration into the precision of a visionary strategist, the proactivity and initiative displayed in innovation, the significance of boundaries akin to the kitchen zone, and the dynamics of rallies have unveiled a wealth of insights that transcend mere metaphor. These insights are the building blocks of effective leadership.

In the world of leadership, much like in the game of pickleball, adaptability is a cornerstone. Leaders must deftly adjust their strategies, pivot when necessary, and remain open to new ideas and perspectives. The finesse required for a well-placed dink shot mirrors the need for finesse in decision-making, ensuring that every action serves a purpose and contributes to the long-term success of the team.

Similarly, embracing innovation, like executing an Ernie shot, demands boldness, quick reflexes, and a willingness to take calculated risks. Leaders who can inspire their teams to embrace innovation can spearhead groundbreaking initiatives and position their organizations for long-term success.

The concept of establishing boundaries, much like the kitchen zone, is paramount in leadership. Effective leaders must set clear expectations, ethical standards, and establish a dynamic playing field where individuals and teams can thrive within established limits.

Furthermore, the art of the rally in pickleball serves as a metaphor for the dynamic and interactive nature of leadership. Leaders must be adept at clear communication, swift decision-making, and the ability to adapt in the face of ever-changing circumstances. Success in both realms hinges on teamwork, creativity, and the ability to persevere in the face of adversity.

These skills cultivated on the pickleball court, from controlled touch to anticipation and adaptability, are not just metaphorical musings. They are the very qualities that underpin effective leadership. As you step off this metaphorical pickleball court and back into the world of leadership, take with you the valuable insights from each chapter. Whether it's the finesse of decision-making or the creativity of the ATP shot, these lessons are your tools for guiding your team to success.

Leadership is an ongoing journey, and your role as a leader is pivotal in shaping the outcome. Keep the spirit of the game alive, lead with confidence, and inspire those around you to achieve greatness. Just as a well-executed pickleball rally can lead to victory, effective leadership can lead to triumph and excellence in your chosen field.

Along our journey, we've encountered a diverse group of individuals, each with their unique experiences, professions, and pickleball stories. These stories serve as compelling examples of how the skills honed on the pickleball court have a profound impact on leadership qualities.

Pam, our corporate executive, ventured into pickleball as a novice and emerged as a visionary strategist, mastering the finesse required for long-term success. Scott, the manager of a cannabis dispensary, unexpectedly found leadership skills in the game's precision, which he successfully applied to his professional role. Yung, a software developer, embraced bold moves and innovation, mirroring his growth as a transformational leader. Brent, a small business owner, used pickleball's kitchen zone as a metaphor to establish boundaries and leadership expectations. Rebecca, the school counselor, discovered resilience through pickleball, becoming an inspiring leader for her students. Irene, a financial service professional, became a collaborative and supportive leader by applying the skills she learned from "poaching." Vince, the engineer, leveraged the second shot's skills to react effectively to challenges in his leadership role.

Each of these stories demonstrates how pickleball, with its unique blend of finesse, strategy, adaptability, and teamwork, shapes individuals into better leaders. Beyond the courts, these individuals have harnessed their newfound skills to navigate the complexities of leadership in their respective fields. Their journeys serve as a powerful reminder that the lessons learned from the pickleball court can be profound catalysts for growth and transformation in leadership roles, underlining the enduring connection between this sport and the art of leadership.

Made in the USA
Las Vegas, NV
03 April 2024

88133883R00066